313 DAYS to
Christmas

313 DAYS to
CHRISTMAS

a human record
of war and imprisonment

Alan Mackay

Argyll
publishing

First published 1998
Argyll Publishing
Glendaruel
Argyll PA22 3AE

ISBN 1 874640 74 2 hardback

Origination
Cordfall Ltd, Glasgow

Printing
St Edmundsbury Press

To my wife Margaret,
my winger for half a century;
to my daughter Alison whose kiss of
life finally brought *313 Days* into being;
and of course to Jack Garrett.

Foreword

Like any successful entrepreneur, Alan Mackay saw a need and thought of a way to fill the gap. This is the story of his Prison Camp wall newspaper, the *Daily Recco*. How he recovered the copies of the paper from the chaos of Germany immediately after the war is a remarkable story in itself.

The Prison of War Camp is a kind of purgatory where men expiate the sin of being captured and prepare themselves for their future lives. They are still at war, duty-bound to harass the enemy, but theirs is a conflict without arms. They belong to a besieged community which exists because of its military character and survives because it reverts to a civilian way of life.

This dichotomy creates problems in determining the form of government. In most British Prison Camps in Germany during the Second World War leadership was automatically assumed by the most senior in rank. There was a military oligarchy.

In the RAF NCOs' camps in which Alan Mackay's *Daily Recco* appeared, a democratic system prevailed. This may have been due to the fact that, in the air, rank did not count.

As the elected leader, I tried to make 'government' as open as possible, but because we were at war there were aspects, security for example, which demanded secrecy and occasions when the camp had to re-adapt itself quickly to service discipline.

Our isolated community, with its barbed wire barriers and the ever-present threat of the gun, could best be likened to a small town in occupied territory, but in many ways it reflected the society we knew. Elected barrack leaders acted as a local council and were assisted by administrative officers. Various committees looked after education, entertainment, the library and sport. The sickbay, though staffed by British doctors, dentists and medical orderlies, and the cooler were, of course, outside our jurisdiction. There was also a powerful, secret, escape committee whose requirements, naturally, had priority over all else. *Tallyho*, to give it its code name, could hardly be democratic but it acted in collaboration with the elected leadership, was careful not to disrupt the ordinary activities of the camp more than was necessary – indeed, encouraged them as a cover for their nefarious doings.

For the most part, the community lived its normal life. There was a flourishing entertainment industry and a thriving 'university', societies catering for diverse interests, a well-attended church. Cigarettes were the camp currency and market forces controlled the economy. There were tycoons, traders, poor men and philanthropists, barbers and bookmakers. Many men followed their professions. There were newspapermen too and Alan Mackay was a particularly youthful one. Yet it was he who saw the opportunity to use his talent.

As Camp Leader, I had to decide whether to allow publication of the *Daily Recco*, as he explains, and it is a privilege now to introduce it to the readers of this book. Many readers no doubt will need no introduction and they will find, as I have, that the mists of memory are lifted. Most of all, I am impressed by the author's sincerity. I am glad the *Daily Recco* has at last come down from the wall.

James A.G. Deans M.B.E.
(1914 – 1989)

Contents

Introduction

I had received a garbled message that a Mr Garret Jack had phoned me and wanted to make contact. I wondered who Mr Garret Jack was – with a name like that he could, I guessed, only be an actor or a theatrical manager. I phoned the number in Edinburgh I had been given and found that I was speaking to New Zealander Jack Garret, a former Prisoner of War with whom I and thousands of others, had shared four years of coexistence in Air Force prisoners' camps during the 1939-45 conflict. He told me that he was leaving the next day for London and a reunion of ex-prisoners and would be delighted to see me that night if that were possible.

Along with me to the meeting with Jack and his wife in Edinburgh I took the bound volumes of the *Daily Recco*, the camp newspaper I had run in two camps in Germany. The idea was to remind Jack of the 'Good Old Days' in the stalags – to refresh his memory regarding the characters with whom we had both shared barrack blocks, traumas, laughs and miseries.

Across the hotel lounge recognition was instant – although we had not seen each other for over thirty years. The drinks flowed, the tales and reminiscences kept pace. Jack kept referring to the '*Reccos*', each new page starting up another series of "You remember. . ." At the end of the night he pleaded with me to be allowed to keep the copies until he had shown them to our fellow Prisoners of War who were to be attending the reunion. Later he returned them with another plea. . . please get them published so that all our old mates can read them, and so that others who were never Prisoners of War can, through their pages, learn something of what life in a Prisoner of War Camp was really like – the day-to-day monotony, the near-starvation, the boredom, the humour. According to Jack, former Camp Leader Dixie Deans and the other ex-Kriegies to whom he had shown the papers were equally keen to see the *Reccos* published as an accurate, daily record of the way life had been for thousands of aircrew who had been shot down and captured.

This book, for which Jack Garret must take the credit – or blame – is an attempt to do just that, to show the way of life of Air Force prisoners all those years ago in Hitler's Third and glorious Reich.

Not that I can remember accurately exactly how it was all those years ago. To me the four years in German Prison Camps contain no actual living colour – the pictures I see in my mind's eye are all in sepia, as through a glass darkly. Through the therapy of nature that blurs the harsh outlines of traumatic experiences and by deliberate personal choice, I had put my four years of captivity behind me. The broad experience could never be forgotten, but the minutiae were lost.

Let me say at once that when the daily newssheet was founded at the beginning of 1943, there was no attempt on my part to record history, nor to make it, although there are some claims now that the *Daily Reccos* deserve a place in the annals of World War II. From barrack block 42N in the RAF Prisoner of War Camp at Sagan, all I was trying to do was my bit to stop the rumours, discontent and frustration which abounded in the camp, from gelling into an explosive mixture which, unchecked, could have created even more frustration. At the same time I was doing something that would help me pass the time and conquer the soul-destroying monotony of Prison Camp life – something to fill in the days which, after two years of captivity, seemed like weeks and the weeks like months.

That is why the *Daily Recco* was born – to purge, through general and open circulation, the cankerous rumours and false reports known to us as *duff gen*, which had invaded and all but taken over the body politic of our Prison Camp in those dark days of Kriegie history when it seemed that being a Kriegie or Prisoner of War was not only a way of life, but life itself.

To every Kriegie (short for the German word *Kriegsgefangener*) Christmas meant two things: 1) the time of parties and presents, family get-togethers, jollity and the old-established order, and 2) the time, we convinced ourselves, when the war would be over and we would be back home in Blighty, New Zealand, Canada, Australia, America or wherever.

In the folly of my youthful exuberance I therefore decided that the newspaper I was about to publish – the only free press in the whole of Nazi-occupied Europe – would carry on its masthead the number of days to Christmas as a daily message of hope. I also decided and my co-editor Bill Butcher agreed, that we would also carry the slogan "Freedom and Boat" a bilingual pun on the German *Freiheit und Brot* (Freedom and Bread) which the Nazis cynically placed along with *Arbeit Macht Frei* (Work brings Freedom) outside the gates of their concentration camps.

And so, on February 15 , l943, the fledgling newssheet, as yet unnamed, carried the words 313 days to Christmas. . . the countdown had begun!

Alan Mackay,
Kirkcaldy, April 1998

Flying High

In 1938, a year before war was declared, I left the Harris Academy in Dundee with my quota of Highers and Lowers and an abundance of soon-to-be-shattered illusions. For the sum of ten shillings a week I sold my labour to the wealthy newspaper/magazine publishing firm of D.C. Thomson, starting as a junior subeditor on the *People's Journal*, a weekly editionised newspaper whose wide circulation throughout Scotland, especially in agricultural communities, had earned it the title of the 'Ploughman's Bible'.

That was the workaday world of 1938 – well distanced from Europe and what was happening in Germany, Austria and Czechoslovakia. The stomp of the jackboot through almost totally defenceless continental countries caused few tremors in Scotland. Paradoxically, it was the Russian aggression against Finland – which I saw in a newsreel in a Dundee cinema – that persuaded me to do my bit for King and Country. I left the Saturday afternoon show and went straight to an RAF recruiting office. I knew that my parents, once I got round to telling them, would understand.

I joined the RAF volunteer reserve, training in the evenings and weekends to be a pilot. The twice-weekly evening lectures were given at Durn, a former mansion on the banks of the River Tay at Perth, with flying – in Tiger Moths – being undertaken at nearby Scone Aerodrome. The flying, all the new recruits agreed, was more enjoyable than the lectures which involved aerodynamics, navigation, map-reading and a study of the intricacies of the internal combustion engine.

Once, after going solo, I managed to stop a Saturday afternoon football match in my native Broughty Ferry, when I went through a routine of amateurish and highly unorthodox aerobatics over the pitch where I knew my father would be a spectator – just so that he could see – and admire – my new found prowess. Fortunately, probably because so many other newly-solo pilots spent the weekends shooting-up their own particular pieces of the countryside round Perth, I escaped without a reprimand from the Scone tutors.

Alan Mackay soon after joining the RAFVR in 1938

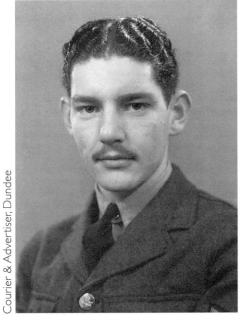

September 1939 and the declaration of war brought escape from the *People's Journal* where at that time I was subbing on the Aberdeen Edition of the paper under the tutelage of white haired, bow-tied, Frank Gray. Little did he know that his training would be partly responsible for the running of the *Daily Recco* and the sudden elevation of his pupil into a fully-fledged editor, reporter, make-up man, compositor, printer, advertising manager *et al*.

But September 1939 did not see all the pilots and observers training at Durn turned into immediate, ready-made front-line forces. We volunteers had seen that a war with Germany was inevitable. But apparently, September 1939 and Hitler's jack-booted march into Poland had caught the Government and top brass completely by surprise. They didn't know what to do with us . . . they had nowhere for us to go.

For about a month, with a daily fruitless search of the mail to see if there was an OHMS letter telling me that I was needed, I enjoyed a government-paid holiday. No call came. The sergeants of the Volunteer Reserve were unwanted. The expertise gained at night classes and Scone Aerodrome was not required. Then the call came – Report to Clare College at Cambridge. We were wanted. We were going to fly. We were going to war.

But it was not to be. Cambridge, where we took over the lodgings, dining rooms – and some of the habits – of the recently-evacuated undergraduates, was simply a marshalling yard where raw civilians were to be turned into disciplined, athletic, fighting aircrew. That was the theory of it. The healthy, athletic end-product was produced by route marches in full kit at 140 steps to the minute, gymnastics, sports, and, of course, square-bashing.

For weeks and months the young men destined to fly, even in those days, expensive and complicated aeroplanes, were taught nothing but how to slope a rifle and do smart about-turns, with the odd lecture thrown in. Staff and pupils learned very quickly that a pint of Guinness from the college buttery at lunchtime brought on a somnolence that overpowered a lecturer's drone and a student's interest. And, despite the drill-induced fitness, meningitis struck – fatally. In our college alone two men died from the virus with similar tallies on the other colleges choc-a-bloc with under-training aircrew. The war, for some of our comrades, was over.

Every morning for days on end, the college quadrangle echoed to the sound of hundreds of young aircrew gargling disinfectant in the battle against the hidden enemy. We stood in ranks, ankle-deep in the snow, wearing only singlets, shorts and boots. Those who survived the virus – and the weather – were healthy. The disinfectant, ejected after gargling with various degrees of feeling – and skill – made pretty purple patches in the snow.

Then, at last, came the posting to an aerodrome – and aeroplanes. At Filton, on the outskirts of Bristol where I was posted along with some of the

Scottish contingent, I saw for the first time that most beautiful of aeroplanes – The Gloster Gladiator. At the other end of the aerodrome to which we were directed there were Tiger Moths. At Filton we learned to fly – again. We learned aerodynamics – again. We learned navigation – again. And for the first time we learned about machine guns, how to assemble and dismantle them – even how to fire them. Our war was getting closer.

At Filton I learned that when removing the retaining clip on the magazine of a Vickers gas-operated K gun, one should always take great care to remove one's thumb from where the clip used to be. Lack of this knowledge cost me a badly gashed thumb, made even worse by a medic who insisted on trying to seal the wound with clips instead of stitches, although any amateur could tell him – and I did – that metal clips bend when they strike bone. At Filton I also learned how to drink Scrumpy – a knowledge gained at the expense of many a double-headed awakening. And I learned that an Austin Swallow, which three of us bought between us, goes like a bomb on pure aviation spirit. We weren't any nearer front-line action but our education was certainly being broadened.

Eventually we left the comfort of our civvy digs at Filton and moved into one-room-to-a-man barracks at Brize Norton where we would, hopefully, gain our wings on either Airspeed Oxfords (for future bomber pilots) or on Harvards (fighters).

Although selected as bomber material, I tried to get the best of both worlds by flying the twin-engined Oxford like a single engined fighter. Taking off after a flight in which my co-trainee Jack Chandler and I had clipped the topmost branches of a tree some distance from the aerodrome – it was a tall tree – I found that the Oxford simply refused to rise off the ground. Our wheels knocked the canopy of a Harvard parked on the airfield perimeter and we ploughed into the field next door.

Examination revealed that the Oxford, its air intakes choked with leaves, was not in a flying condition. Jack and I managed to remove the offending leaves before the arrival of breathless ground crew, a fire engine and the blood wagon.

Marched in front of the C.O. and charged with the Air Force equivalent of careless driving, I was warned that the cost of the aircraft – £15,000 which was a staggering sum at that time – could be deducted from my pay. The groundcrew escort who had marched me in and who now stood stiffly to attention on either side of me, kept me upright. Given a severe – and deserved – wigging, I was sent back to my barracks with my tail between my legs. Later I was presented by the same C.O. with my wings. I was a pilot at last.

O for Orange

My next posting was to Bassingbourne to learn how to fly Vickers Wellingtons, known affectionately to one and all as Wimpys from the Popeye cartoon character, J Wellington Wimpy. Despite its size – it seemed to take half a day to walk from nose to tail – the Wimpy handled as easily and sweetly as a Tiger Moth, the only worrying feature being the way its wingtips fluttered when the plane was pulled out of a tight turn. A crisscross of steel on the geodetic principle covered in doped canvas, Wimpys survived a great deal of punishment, often flying home from raids with large holes in the sides and with tattered fabric trailing like a proud pennant as amazed and grateful crews lobbed down on their home dromes. I was to learn later that they cost £30,000 each.

At Bassingbourne we crewed-up – six complete strangers thrust together to be welded into an efficient fighting unit. My second pilot was Leonard Millington, known as Millie; the front gunner Bill Ainsworth; navigator George McRiner; wireless operator Jim House and rear gunner New Zealander Steve Bevan. We flew by day and by night, learning the aircraft, learning how to drop bombs on target, how to fire our guns at practice drogues towed by Fairey Battles, how to get along with each other and how to trust each others' capabilities. We worked hard and we had pride in our work. We were ready for war.

And then, just after my twentieth birthday on November 5, 1940, we were posted to No 9 Squadron at Honington. Immediately, lifelong friendships were struck up with roommates and other crews. With a bit of luck lifelong could mean a month. Then, with the non-return from an operation of a friend or roommate, a share-out would take place of the best of his uniform and whatever he had left of a parcel from home. The share-out was made in an atmosphere of 'it could be my stuff that goes next'. One character, reported to be shot down over the Channel when on his way home from a raid on Germany, fooled us all by turning up at Honington a week later. There was a mad scurry to return to him the pieces of uniform that had been reallocated among his friends. What he never saw again was the rich, home-made cake he had been saving up for Christmas.

New Zealander, Steve Bevan, took the precarious Rear Gunner role in the Vickers Wellington. Later, whilst a Prisoner of War, Alan Mackay wrote a poem (below)

Rear Gunner
He said, "I'm done," then coughed.
I saw the red drops fall
On mask; the oxygen hissed,
Then blood – congealed, its task completed,
Stopped.
OK he sighed, and smiled.
Heaven was there, with Courage,
Thumb to nose to utter Hell.
The fighter, flame-wrapped,
Smoke-trailing – a funeral pyre;
Lurid, stinging flames lit him,
Etching horror, pain –
Deep-carved
Tight-lipped,
But never fear.

Most aircrew expected to be killed – many of those in this 1940 picture of crews at Bassingbourne were killed or captured

© Vickers Wellington bombers flying in formation

© RAF Museum, Hendon Ref P3357

After three ops as a second pilot or Second Dickie I was given my own aeroplane. Our code was O for Orange . . . we would have preferred P for Relief!

Operations, we found to the credit of the instructors on the conversion course, were much the same as night exercises with danger and excitement added. What was – illogically – annoying, was being shot at when over the friendly territories of France, Belgium and Holland on the way to Germany. Even less like cricket was being shot at – with accuracy and venom – on the nights we dropped nothing but leaflets on the countryside and towns below. Our reaction to being shot at on those occasions was to leave some of the leaflets still in bundles in the hope that someone would at least get a sore head when they landed.

Briefings for operations were a mixture of good and bad. The good was that the weather reports were, mostly, accurate – there was always weather. The bad was that sometimes we were told that barrage balloon cables over the target were stretching 15,000 feet into the night sky – 3,000 feet above our operational level with the result that we stood a very good chance of crashing into them.

And bad was the information we got one night that our target was the Post Office at Hanover, a target, we were told, because vital information was being sent through the postal services by the Germans and that it would be in Hanover Post Office at the time our bombs were due to fall. The fact that the Post Office in Hanover, as in most other towns, was in a heavily built-up area in the centre of town inhabited by civilians, was not supposed to occur to us.

Bad too, was the scant information we were given about what to do if we survived being shot down. Most of us expected to be killed. That is why, probably, we were not too worried about the lack of information on how to survive, how to contact resistance groups and how to get home after landing in enemy territory. We received with thanks the front collar studs which had compasses concealed in the base. We did not ask for more.

Vickers Wellingtons in training over Stradishall, 1939

OUVRIERS FRANÇAIS,
VOICI L'AVENIR QUE VOUS RESERVENT VOS MAITRES ALLEMANDS!

ON vous a répété souvent que la France a perdu la guerre parceque vous n'avez pas assez travaillé. Le ...ier Baudouin, qui souffle ces idées au gouvernement de Vichy, oublie sans doute que vous avez accepté spontanément de porter la semaine de travail de 40 heures à 60 heures ou davantage, dès que vous avez su que le salut du pays était en jeu. Il oublie que vous auriez accepté bien d'autres efforts pour augmenter la production, pour préserver votre liberté et celle de la France.

Le gouvernement de Vichy vous dit aujourd'hui qu'il faut diminuer la production industrielle de la France. Ainsi, les mêmes hommes qui vous reprochaient hier de ne pas avoir fourni un effort suffisant, veulent aujourd'hui supprimer votre profession et vous envoyer à la terre.

Le gouvernement de Vichy vous parle aussi de réformes, et de reconstruction nationale. En fait, les réformes faites depuis un siècle en France ont été conquises en grande partie par vos groupements. Au nom d'un ordre nouveau, on s'apprête à les supprimer et à vous priver de vos droits.

En vérité, que ce soit le gouvernement de Vichy, ou la presse de Paris, ou la radio qui demandent ces réformes, que les projets soient signés Belin, Abetz ou Doriot, peu importe :

C'EST TOUJOURS HITLER QUI COMMANDE

Hitler veut :

1. Faire de la France un pays agricole, comme au moyen âge. Ainsi il supprimerait la concurrence industrielle française et la France serait forcée d'acheter les produits allemands. Vous perdriez dans l'opération tout le bénéfice de vos années d'apprentissage et de la connaissance de votre métier. Votre standard de vie sera abaissé. Les organisations de défense ouvrière seront anéanties. Vous ne pourrez plus choisir votre métier: Hitler le choisira pour vous.

2. Hitler ne laissera subsister qu'un petit nombre d'industries françaises. Quelques centaines de milliers d'ouvriers pourront

34

peut-être y trouver des emplois. Mais leurs conditions de vie seront maintenues, systématiquement, au-dessous de celles de l'ouvrier allemand. A la place de vos syndicats, vous aurez, comme en Allemagne, l'autorité d'un 'Front de Travail' qui exigera de vous l'obéissance absolue, qui fera de vous des esclaves. Toute révolte sera punie du camp de concentration.

3. Hitler a besoin d'armements. Il maintient donc provisoirement certaines industries françaises qui travaillent pour la guerre.

Avant de vous y engager, ...chissez: ces usines travaillent pour prolonger la guerre, pour la victoire des Nazis. Ces usines subiront jour après jour les bombardements de l'aviation anglaise. Vous ne voudrez pas risquer votre vie pour aider Hitler.

ON VEUT ASSERVIR L'OUVRIER FRANÇAIS

—comme a été asservi l'ouvrier d'Autriche, de Tchécoslovaquie, de Pologne, de Belgique, de Hollande. Les Allemands se réservent les bénéfices industriels, le confort, les instruments de domination. Ils vous laissent la misère, les heures de travail interminables, la nourriture insuffisante.

Travailleurs français, ... avez dans le sang le goût de la liberté. Les peuples d'Europe ne supporteront pas indéfiniment l'esclavage, et la France, pays de la Révolution, encore moins que les autres.

Ce n'est pas vous qui pourriez vous résigner ou vous abandonner au désespoir. Maintenant moins que jamais. Déjà l'ennemi, bafoué par l'échec de ses plans d'invasion de l'Angleterre, donne des signes d'inquiétude. Déjà il voit s'approcher l'heure du châtiment.

Ouvriers français, vous pouvez contribuer à hâter cette heure. Vous n'êtes pas seuls. Toute une série d'autres peuples européens, momentanément asservis par le même tyran, partagent vos souffrances, mais aussi votre amertume, votre amour de la liberté et votre volonté de secouer le joug.

Les armées britanniques et les Forces Françaises libres sont là, aux côtés de celles des autres Alliés. Vous pouvez compter sur elles. Elles combattent pour vous délivrer de même que tous les peuples opprimés d'Europe. Elles ne connaîtront ni paix ni repos tant que la tyrannie hitlérienne qui vous réduit à l'esclavage ne sera pas détruite. Ayez confiance.

LA VICTOIRE EST MOINS ELOIGNEE QUE VOUS N'OSEZ ESPERER

For You the War is Over

Surprised by the fact that we had lasted on the squadron longer than most – in those days a month was the average life-expectancy of a bomber crew – we volunteered for a daylight low-level attack on Gelsenkirchen, an oil refinery town on the Ruhr. Night attacks had repeatedly failed to knock out the oil installation which was vital to Germany's war effort and which was protected by a satellite replica, complete with tempting street lights and mock fires, situated a comfortable distance away on open heath. This satellite, according to recce pictures taken in daylight on the morning after a night raid, had frequently been hit instead of the refineries themselves. Our offer was declined by the Squadron Commander.

A month later, returning from a raid on Germany on the night of February 11/12, we were down to 1,000 feet crossing the North Sea en route to Honington, debriefing and a mug of coffee laced with rum. Lights and gun flashes dead ahead indicated that the Suffolk coast was being pasted by German bombers. Behind the flashes the cool white fingers of searchlights probed and stroked the black velvet of the sky.

George McRiner calculated that, while we were ten minutes flying time away from the lights, the coast was still twenty minutes distant. Bill Ainsworth in the front turret gave his considered opinion that the navigator was off his chump – the lights and the coast were approaching at a rapid rate of knots.

The argument was settled when, through a gap in the clouds, we saw the coastline still some distance away – and a convoy of British ships under attack directly beneath us. Shells ripped through the fragile fabric of 'O for Orange'.

Millie shot off the colour of the day with a Verey pistol to let the Navy below know that we were friendly – or had been until they shot at us. By the light of the flare which would, hopefully, guarantee our safety from any more Navy shells, the German convoy raider switched his guns to us. The starboard engine packed in. We ploughed up three fields on the Suffolk coast with the only injury being a twisted leg sustained by Millie.

(Opposite)
A leaflet of the type dropped over Allied France, Belgium and Holland – crews were still shot at!

Woebegone and shattered, we gathered ourselves and our belongings together and trudged towards the nearest building and, we hoped, comfort. We came to a mansion standing on its own. Eventually there was a response to our banging on the front door – the owner trained a double-barrelled shotgun on us from an upstairs window. Persuaded that we were stranded British and not German fliers, he reluctantly opened the door and invited us in – provided we first of all removed our muddy flying boots so that his carpets would not get soiled. So much for English hospitality.

After another couple of ops we were told that the posting to North Africa we had requested was on. Alan Butler, one of the 9 Squadron Observers, volunteered to go with us in place of George McRiner who had opted to stay in Blighty. Butler, who became the oldest member of the crew, wanted, like us, to swap the grim English winter for the sunshine of the Middle East and to experience "something different". That he did. In memoirs published after the war, he wrote that the "different" was dicing with death twice in two days. He was kind enough to state that he owed me an "everlasting debt" for twice saving his life.

We were given embarcation leave and then reported to Stradishall to pick up a brand-new plane for transit to Malta. A serious malfunction just after takeoff from Stradishall en route to the Mediterranean island gave us a few hairy moments before we got safely back to the deck. The next day, with the aircraft repaired, we were told that Malta, in the process of earning its George Cross, was off the visiting list. The island, with its aerodrome at Luqa being pounded day and night by German and Italian bombers despite the valiant defence put up by three Gloster Gladiators named Faith, Hope and Charity, was off limits! Instead we were nominated to be the first-ever crew to attempt England to North Africa nonstop. Benghazi was our destination. They took out some of the spare parts and mail we were carrying to the Desert Rats in Africa. They gave us extra fuel instead. It was the night of March 10/11 1941 – just under a month since we had first been shot down.

We left a cold England at 8 o'clock at night with an estimated time of arrival at Benghazi of 8am the next morning. The flight, apart from being shot at over France as we winged our way to the sunny south, was uneventful. Then from the front turret Bill Ainsworth reported lights – hundreds of them. We had never before seen a whole town lit up at night. The neutral Swiss town, with its street and house lights blazing, was like a wonderland – the only lights we had seen in Britain were flarepaths or fire-raddled targets. We made a course correction and droned on. Suddenly a red ball shot up past the nose of the kite. My immediate reaction as I yanked the wheel and kicked the rudder in an instinctive avoiding action was who the hell is shooting at us down here? The red ball grew larger. It was the sun. But it was sunrise like none we had ever seen before – someone should have warned us.

For you the war is over!
Sgt Jim House being offered bread and coffee by a German captor on the North African beach where they had been shot down. Alan Mackay is next in the background

Another beach photo

The prisoners are driven off on their journey to POW camp

These photographs appeared in German newspapers

So it was daylight when we hit the coast of North Africa. The bay down below didn't look the way the Bay at Benghazi should – we were too far to the North. But not to worry. We had been told before leaving England the previous night that the Eighth Army held all that part of the coast. That was when the first shell hit us. More then came from that unfriendly shoreline and an ME 110 joined in the attack on us. Steve in the rear turret did his best to blast it out of the sky. But it was our Wimpy that was shot down – right beside Mussolini's marble arch through which, only hours before, the British army had retreated on their way back to Benghazi and Cairo. We ploughed up a considerable stretch of the beach. Thinking back to Brize Norton and the previous month's convoy incident, I ruefully decided that I should have been a farmer.

As we stood beside the burnt-out Wimpy a swaggering German Officer approached. In almost perfect English he said, "For you the war is over."

They parked us on the sand dunes while they decided what to do with us. The German soldiers in their distinctive Afrika Corps uniforms gave us bread (hard and black), meat (tinned and coarse) and from their water bottles a drink (it turned out to be red wine). Our fur-lined flying suits discarded, we sat in the blazing sun, getting redder and redder. One by one we were taken a short distance away for interrogation. One by one we told the English-speaking officer that we had been in Africa for months, that we had been returning from a raid on Italy when we were shot down. The officer, looking at our beet-red faces, was not convinced. But he was polite about it.

Eventually we were loaded into an open car and driven to Tripoli. I had my flying scarf wrapped round my head turban fashion, but it did not completely shield me from the sun – that was just another part of the discomfort, the discomfiture, the agony of being a Prisoner of War.

That first night of captivity in Tripoli was the worst of my life – then or since. I was a prisoner. I was surrounded by an armed and unknown enemy. I was in solitary confinement in a camel stable. The previous tenant had gone, but his stench lingered on. The camp bed in the middle of the floor was a makeshift contraption with a piece of old carpet instead of canvas, stretched out none too tightly on a wooden frame. During the night my fitful tossing and turning ripped it from end to end. I was miserable.

The next morning the crew – by their looks they had suffered as well – was reassembled. We were watered and fed, just like the camels, then driven to the aerodrome. Waiting for us was a Junkers 52. It was the first time I had seen a plane with three engines and corrugated sides. Inside it had a different smell. Different makes of planes like different makes of cars have a smell peculiar to their manufacture. The Junkers had a stronger, entirely different smell compared to any British plane. It too convinced me that from now on everything was going to be – different.

We flew to Sicily, spending a night in a hilltop fortress, then flew the next day to Bari on the heel of Italy – up to the north and then over the Alps to Germany. Noticeable at all the stops we made en route was the foppishness – and courtesy – of the Italian Officers and the way they took orders yelled at them by our guards who ranked no higher than a Sgt. Major. It was patently obvious who were the topdogs and who was running the war in this part of the world. It was definitely not a case of allies, but of master and servant – even slave.

At Frankfurt-am-Main our army transit guards handed us over to the Luftwaffe, their blue airman's uniforms almost matching ours – apart from the cut. We were driven in an open car through the city streets, past pavement-lining crowds who had obviously been advised that a Prisoner of War show was being laid on for them. They were not friendly. At Oberursel, a tiny hamlet clinging to the wooded side of a hill above the town, we saw our first barbed wire compound; we were home.

But we did not join the figures we could see behind the barbed wire of Dulag Luft, the Air Force prisoners reception centre. We were led to a three-storey building and placed into individual cells. Through the barred window I could see a white-painted house across the road which led into the camp. During the week I spent in solitary I watched the daily routine of a young girl who started every morning by laying her eiderdown over the window sill. Through her open window I could hear – every day – the Woody Woodpecker song, played loud and clear. It went to the bottom of my hit parade.

Every day, two German officers entered the room – with questionnaires. I gave my name, rank and number. They gave me Scotch Whisky and Gold Flake cigarettes – captured at Dunkirk, they boasted proudly. They said that they knew that I belonged to 9 Squadron and listed a whole number of officers and crews based at Honington when I had been there.

Breaking the name, rank and number rule, I took great delight in telling them – with conviction – that I did not belong to 9 Squadron. But I wondered at the accuracy of their information which, as far as my own crew was concerned, was only a matter of a few weeks out of date. On other occasions the officers entered with civilians. Explaining that the civilians were Red Cross officials, the officers then bowed and left – to allow us, so they said, to speak freely with the Red Cross representatives. But the civilians asked the same questions as the officers. They too were given the name, rank and number routine.

Eventually we were allowed out of solitary and taken to the main compound to join the other prisoners. The spell in solitary had made us hypersensitive and suspicious so that the Senior British Officer at Dulag Luft – Wing Commander Day – got only the name, rank and number answers when, walking round the compound and explaining the working of the camp and its routine, he asked how things were back home, what Squadron we were from, how the war was going and how and where we had been shot down. It was only when we met former Squadron mates who had been shot down earlier, that we relaxed enough to talk about our own disaster.

At Dulag Luft while we waited to be sent to a real Prisoner of War Camp, we were given the opportunity of – provided we gave our parole that we would not try to escape – going for walks in the woods above the village of Oberursel. Working on the principle that we might be able to spy out the lay of the land for a later escape attempt, we agreed. Under the charge of one officer and two armed guards, groups of about twenty prisoners at a time would meander along the forest walks. Years later, when I returned to other parts of Germany and walked through other woods, the scent of the firs and pines would bring back instant memories of youth, Dulag Luft and Woody Woodpecker.

Eventually we were paraded and told that we were to be sent to Barth in Pomerania. Apart from knowing that it was where a certain breed of dog came from, we hadn't a clue where either Barth or Pomerania was. We learned throughout that summer and long cold winter that Barth is a seaport on the Baltic and that, in winter, the Baltic freezes over – completely.

Kriegies

The journey to Barth, with frequent stops in sidings to allow more important military traffic through, was made by rail in conventional type carriages. It was to be the last journey we made in such comparative comfort. Future transfers from camp to camp were made in cattle trucks, most of them purloined from the French railway system and bearing the legend *40 hommes / 8 chevaux*. Travelling with thirty-nine other men in a bare wooden truck with a pungent, frequently overflowing bucket slopping its noisome contents at every set of points, would never have been approved by Baedecker. We didn't approve either.

The camp at Barth was sited on the edge of the almost obligatory forest. The single-storey wooden barracks were, like everything German, laid out in orderly fashion. The only odd thing about them was that they stood on small brick-built pillars some two feet off the ground. This we were warned, was so that any tunnelling under the floors could be easily spotted by the German security guards or Ferrets who generally wore black overalls and frowns. The floors of the barracks were united to the pillars by angle-irons some two inches broad. These, we discovered, made almost perfect ice skates. Coached by Canadian prisoners and using ingeniously-contrived sticks, we played ice hockey or just generally sported about on the ice which seemed to last for months. Meantime the huts, unbalanced by the loss of the majority of their underpinnings, sagged badly. The Germans were not amused.

The camp itself was divided into compounds which were self-contained units, separating the officers from the NCOs, the prisoners from the German administrative staff and later the British from the Russians and Americans. Each compound was surrounded by double thickness barbed wire fences about ten feet high and with coiled barbed wire rolls in between. And between the prisoners and the first of the wire fences was a knee-high warning wire. Anyone moving between the warning wire and the fence was liable to be shot at – and killed – by the guards who patrolled on the outside of the double fence or stood, with machine guns at the ready, in the wooden watch towers built every so many yards round the whole camp.

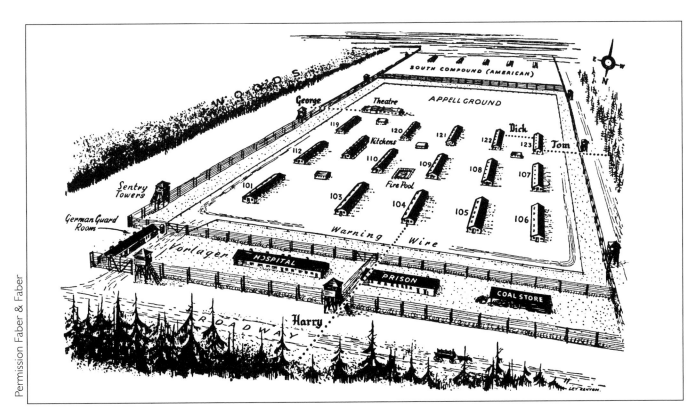

The officers' compound in the camp at Sagan. This diagram is taken from the book The Great Escape and shows the routes of the planned escape tunnels, code-named Tom, Dick and Harry

Each barrack block housed between 150 and 200 men. Each had a toilet and wash room at one end and cooking facilities at the other. The barrack leader had his quarters near the cooking end – a perk which was not grudged by prisoners too lazy to take on any position of responsibility within the camp.

Sleeping accommodation consisted of two-tier wooden beds whose wooden-slatted bases became, in the long winter months, a prime source of the fuel vital to keep body and soul together. A few tables and stools were provided by our hosts. As time went by and prisoner ingenuity increased as necessity truly mothered invention, armchairs, cupboards and other furniture decorated the barracks of long-established Kriegies.

Out in the communal world of the compound, large wash barracks provided cold water for personal hygiene and the dhobying by which prisoners made their clothes presentable – more or less. There were also special barracks known as the thunder boxes which housed the toilets in, dependent on local style, either twenty or one hundred seats in line – a style of building which, while contributing nothing to modesty, allowed the continuation of an argument or friendly discussion while nature was being satisfied. The toilets were emptied by a horse-drawn tank – and one man. Placing a hose from his tank into the nearest thunder box aperture, he would then stand contentedly puffing away at his pipe for a matter of minutes. His estimation of time and quantity to be siphoned off was immaculate. At the precise moment when there was sufficient gas in his empty tank he would, taking another match, light it and hold it at a tiny valve opening at the top of the tank. Natural science did the rest as with a whoosh the contents of the thunderboxes would be transferred to the tank. Not so pleasant was the next stage in the thrifty German process. The tank load would be sprayed on the fields round the camp to pave the way for a bumper crop of vegetables.

Outside the compound but still part of the camp and still within the wire was the *Vorlager* – the blocks containing the German administration offices, their barracks, the camp sick bay, Red Cross stores and the 'cooler', the specially-designed cell block for delinquent prisoners. A spell in the cooler could be earned by something as serious as an escape attempt or as trivial as playing games on *Appell*, the twice-daily roll calls which the Germans stretched out because of their apparent inability to count, although in some cases the prisoners deliberately made their task more difficult.

I was to spend four days in the cooler after the failure of an admittedly cheeky escape attempt, in which, dressed like a German Guard I was to lead two fellow Kriegies on a working party out of the compound, through the *Vorlager* and so to freedom. I was wearing Red Cross issue pyjamas which closely resembled the Guard's summertime fatigue uniforms. It was made more authentic by a German roundel on my RAF forage cap and the addition of a boot-polish stained cardboard belt and gun holster. We were detected at the gate into the *Vorlager* when the Kommandant, accompanied by staff and a squad of goons, arrived at the gate at the same time. The Kommandant was in the process of calling the whole camp on parade so that he could hand out some special information. The goons were there to go through the barracks looking for contraband and other escape paraphernalia while the speechifying was going on. After that abortive escapade I made one other escape attempt, this time by the more conventional tunnel – that effort failed when the tunnel collapsed.

After the initial settling-in period at Barth where compatible groups of prisoners gathered together in certain huts, turning their new quarters into self-contained little worlds, some of us started preparing ourselves for life after the war – which was about to end at Christmas. Prisoners studied, learned languages, carved, developed hobbies and interests. And inevitably, they quarrelled and argued and fought although, generally, punch-ups were far less common than might have been expected. We were learning the art of tolerance.

These RAF camps consisting, like aircrews, mostly of sergeants, were concentrations of young, in the UK sense, middle-class men whose flying experiences together had turned them into independent and interdependent spirits with a highly-developed sense of justice and fairness. And in the chaos of a world war, the trauma of being shot down, the terrible reality of being no longer free and the rigours of captivity, they forged a unity and level-headedness, a stoicism big enough, durable enough, to see them through the darkest days of their lives. They became organised. They ran their own affairs with the blessing of successive

German Kommandants. They were a practical practising democracy in the middle of a Fascist empire, subject occasionally to outbursts of Nazi brutality, bloody-mindedness and authoritarianism. The Stalag Lufts or Air Force camps were, unlike the Air Force with its "Officers and Other Ranks" mentality, a completely classless society. Camp rationale was: 1) surviving; 2) escape; and 3) getting by. Seniority was not by rank but, largely, by the time spent as a Prisoner of War. "Get some in", meaning days, weeks, years in captivity, was used as a downgrading means of putting new and recent arrivals in the camp at the bottom of the Lager's social structure – a dichotomy which showed that even equality had its degrees of equalness!

It was at Barth that we saw our first Russian prisoners – the first victims of Hitler's Operation Barbarossa. Woebegone, unkempt, with tattered, paper-thin uniforms and generally with cloth rags in place of footwear, they looked as if they had marched all the way from Russia – perhaps they had. The Germans, already notorious for their treatment of the Jews as sub-humans, treated the Russians in the same way – or worse. One day as a line of Russian prisoners was marched past our wire on the way to their segregated compound, we threw hunks of our precious bread ration to them. One man, struck on the head by a quarter loaf, fell – stunned. It was either a comment on his condition or on the quality of the bread.

The winter, with the well-worn track around the perimeter of the compound becoming in succession a muddy quagmire, a snow-covered wilderness and a frozen-solid, ankle-twisting rutted booby-trap, wore on. One day the camp buzzed to the news brought in by a guard, that one of his mates, out courting a local girl, had been found with her in the morning – both dead, both frozen *in flagrante-* icicles. The comments varied from "poor bugger" to "what a way to die".

The cold was everywhere. We lived with it by day and we took it to bed with us at night. Fuel was a major problem. Occasionally the Germans would supply us with briquettes for use in the communal stoves that were the hubs of intellectual and social life in each barrack. Occasionally they would organise wood parties which, with the inevitable guards, were led to the nearby forest to forage for sticks, branches and, if the guards were amenable, whole trees. But the staple firewood came from the bed-boards on the two-tier bunks. Each prisoner was allocated a bed, enough boards to stretch from end to end and a palliasse filled with corn chaff or wood shavings. As the winter drew out, the boards shrank in what could probably be calculated as an exact formula relating air temperature to wood-generated heat. By spring most prisoners were sleeping on the minimum number of boards required to keep their palliasses from falling down on to their bunkmates underneath or on to the floor.

Sticking more or less to the Geneva Convention relating to Prisoners of War which stipulated that they should spend no more that one year in any

"Keeps talking about bed boards or somethin'"

For some spring came too late – as ably illustrated two years later by our tame cartoonist in the Daily Recco

The camp at Sagan
Some Kriegies spent their waking
hours dreaming up and occasionally
putting into practice, escape ideas.
Sagan was the location for one of the
biggest prisoner break-outs of World
War II on the night of 24th March
1944. Of the prisoners who escaped, 50
were shot by the Germans. These
events were depicted in the book, The
Great Escape, later made into a film

particular camp, the Germans moved us from Barth to Sagan. This was a
virgin camp, not only sited beside a forest, but created from one with tree
stumps still liberally covering the area designated as our sports field.

To help us clear the site so that we could play football and other games, the
Germans supplied us with block, tackle and chains plus a tripod to pull the
stumps out. The rest was up to us. But although removing the stumps was
in our own interest, the Kriegies took their time about the job. Frequently,
frustrated by the slowness of progress, the guards would drop their rifles
and wade in to the work, showing us how it should be done. The keenness
to work was one of the better German characteristics.

Sagan, because of its former forest flooring, was an ideal camp for
tunnelling. At one time practically every block in the camp had a tunnel at
some stage of construction under the floorboards. Especially favoured were
the wash and latrine blocks which were nearest the boundary wire and
freedom. Almost every week prisoners were sent to the cooler when their
particular tunnel was unearthed by the ferrets. While some Kriegies spent
their waking hours dreaming up and occasionally putting into practice,
escape ideas, others concentrated on equipping themselves for the future,
studying, and even sitting exams while the camp life flowed around them.
Others just spent the time filling-in time. Some made a career of bitching
about everything. Some took their own personal way out of a life which
had become unbearable – one by cutting his throat in a wash-house loft;
another by trying to climb the wire in broad daylight. Their deaths affected
the whole camp. Morale sank.

The Birth of the *Recco*

In spring, a young man's fancy lightly turns to thoughts of . . . what an old Kriegie has been thinking about all winter long – and longer. But it wasn't spring yet. February 1943 was still cold and wet and miserable. And, as Kriegies had come to learn, in Germany the cold was colder, the wind sharper, the snow wetter, the rain more persistent and the mud muddier.

In winter the call to morning *Appell* meant, in addition to standing about in ankle-deep mud on the parade ground, standing about in boots still wet from roll-call the previous evening.

Winter too, meant that for more hours than usual, people were forced into a state of close companionship. Even the limited freedom of walking around the compound was denied us by the weather and the freedom of wandering into other barracks was denied by the locking up after an early curfew. So we were forced in upon ourselves, and each other. Regional accents, at one time novel and even endearing, grated against exposed sensitivities. Physical contact, an inescapable part of life lived in a battery-hen environment, became something to be avoided . . . usually at the cost of a broken friendship. And while the prisoner became thin through the usual feeding which always deteriorated in winter – or at least seemed to – rumours grew fat like the maggots we were once served along with rotten horseflesh after bombs had wrecked a neighbouring German food depot.

While Kriegies huddled in a multicoloured multitude of clothing in an attempt to keep warm, discontent flourished like a hothouse plant. Envy, suspicion, bitterness, jealousy and plain animosity separated man from man and group from group. Graft, favouritism and corruption were claimed – and denied. That's the way it was the winter before the *Daily Recco* was born. Sagan, with another Home for Christmas missed, was not a happy place.

While notices were pinned on barrack blocks giving information about lectures, recitals, sports, shows, etc, there was nothing giving a global picture of all the activities through which the Kriegies sought relief from the deadly, daily boredom. There was no forum where moans could be expressed – and answered. That was when I made two rash decisions. One was that I would run a camp newspaper, and the second was that it would be laid out like a newspaper, not just a collection of varied items of information relating to societies, meetings and entertainment. In walks round the compound I persuaded roommate Bill Butcher that it was a good idea, and that, more importantly, he could help with the donkey-work of actually writing the pages – if and when we got approval for the project from Camp Leader, Dixie Deans. Bill, agreeing that it would help pass the time for him as well and not realising just how much time it would pass, said yes, he would help.

Full of youthful enthusiasm, I took the idea to Dixie. He was far from enamoured by the proposition – for a variety of reasons. One of his fears was that I might, inadvertently, print some item of war news which could have come only from the camp's illegal radio, so brilliantly manufactured by Curly Bristow and so diligently sought by the German guards in frequent searches. The radio was the camp's most cherished possession. It had cost many hours of secret work and much in the way of cigarettes, chocolate, soap and other inducements surreptitiously passed to German guards in exchange for valves and other parts – guards who risked imprisonment and even death by their actions. The radio, argued Dixie, was our most important link with the outside world, giving news and reports which had not first passed through the distortions of the Nazi propaganda machine. The radio must be protected at all costs.

I managed to persuade Dixie that a newspaper might possibly help instead of hinder that purpose. I suggested that if we printed, from time to time, items taken from the German newspapers which circulated within the camp, then even the Germans would realise that by printing their news, we could not possibly have access to any other information. Dixie also agreed that morale might be helped by an even more open form of government being shown through publication of camp affairs. But first, he said, he had to get the approval of the Kommandant and the release to us of paper, ink and other materials. This he did and work began on the first issue. The sheet, handwritten against a background of ribald and facetious comment from our roommates in barrack 42N, was prepared on a table frequently jostled by fellow prisoners preparing and eating their evening meal at the other end. It was written to the background noise of a scratchy gramophone record (all our records were scratchy) and it was written despite the shoulder-nudging by people who wanted to be the first to see the new baby.

The first edition of the then unnamed brain child (a prize of 50 cigarettes was offered for a title) carried across the centre spread our *raison d'etre* and a declaration of our editorial intentions.

Introducing Us to You

The first edition was on February 15th, 1943, and two days later the paper, which had not really aspired to have a name, was entitled the *Daily Recco*. The title came from Tubby Dixon who normally passed his time writing plays for the camp theatre. He thought that a daily reconnaissance of the camp was what we were about.

We decided that each issue of the *Recco* should carry across the top, the address of the editorial offices – block 42N; the paper's slogan *Freiheit und Brot* which translated into Freedom and Bread; the current date and the reminder that each day was so many days to Christmas – the Christmas we were always sure we would be home by.

The baby thrived. Kind uncles presented it – almost daily – with gifts of ideas. Readers at the end of the block where the paper was pinned up every morning, jostled with each other to read the immortal prose, some rescued it when it was blown down ... souvenir hunters even pinched the odd copy.

During the last few days we have heard various subterranean murmurings. These murmurings culminated in questions of Why and What: Why don't we know what is happening to so and so? Why don't we know what is going on? Why was such and such kept dark? What was the result of such a thing and how does it affect us? As a result of this it was decided to start a daily news-sheet with the following aims: –

1. To present the news of the day without bias or distortion.

2. To give concise reports of meetings which affect the compound.

3. To squash, if possible, all malignant rumours.

4. To give up-to-the-minute "gen" on the Red Cross, Sport, Entertainment and other matters in which you are interested.

5. To shed light on the swift moving stream in and out of jail and the reasons thereof.

In conclusion, remember that we depend upon you for the news. If you have any queries, ideas or information, bring it to Mackay and Butcher, Block 42.N.

Death of the Holiday Camp

By dint of a great deal of ingenuity, hard work, patience, skill, plus large quantities of graft, bribery and cajolery involving German guards, some of the prisoners had made elaborate stage sets and costumes which, from the back of a smoke-filled hall, looked as good as anything on the West End stage.

The German propaganda machine, never slow to take advantage, used the stage backdrops as backcloths for group photographs of the Kriegies who could then buy the postcard-size snap to send home. The prisoners, delighted to give pictorial reassurance to their loved ones that they were more or less hale and likewise hearty, sent the snaps back to Blighty.

The words they used when sending the snaps home were their own. And some, it appeared from extracts we received in letters back from the UK, must have been shooting a hell of a line – possibly in an attempt to make light of their misfortunes. No-one in the camp was against fellow prisoners giving relatives and loved ones a rosier-than-real picture of life in a Stalag Luft. We all did it. But some, obviously, had painted an entirely false picture of Kriegie life. The *Recco* decided that enough was enough and the false information, seemingly widely broadcast in the special POW magazine prepared in the UK for the relatives of prisoners, had to stop.

The gentle rebuke in our second issue, (see opposite) dated February 16, appeared to bear fruit. But in later editions we had to revert to our call for care to be taken in what was written home. Like the rest of the prisoners we made light of our conditions in letters, but beer gardens, swimming pools and dance bands going on tour was just too much.

The German propaganda machine, never slow to take advantage, used stage backdrops made by prisoners as backcloths for group photographs. Prisoners could then buy the postcard-size snap to send home. Pictured here were a group of Scots POWs:
(back row) Sgts. Mackay, McIntosh, McCreary, Trundle, Stirling, Baird & Younger;
(front row) Sgts. Houston, Hastie, Fotheringham, Robertson & McDonald

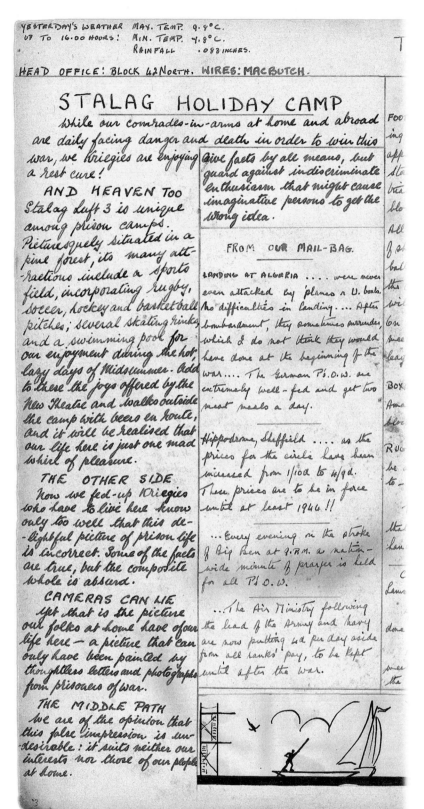

STALAG HOLIDAY CAMP

While our comrades-in-arms at home and abroad are daily facing danger and death in order to win this war, we Kriegies are enjoying a rest cure!

And heaven too

Stalag Luft 3 is unique among prison camps. Picturesquely situated in a pine forest, its many attractions include a sports field, incorporating rugby, soccer, hockey and basketball pitches; several skating rinks, and a swimming pool for our enjoyment during the hot lazy days of Midsummer. Add to these the joys offered by the New Theatre and walks outside the camp with beers en route, and it will be realised that our life here is just one mad whirl of pleasure.

The other side

Now we fed-up Kriegies who have to live here know only too well that this delightful picture of prison life is incorrect. Some of the facts are true, but the composite whole is absurd.

Cameras can lie

Yet that is the picture our folks at home have of our life here – a picture that can only have been painted by thoughtless letters and photographs from prisoners of war.

The middle path

We are of the opinion that this false impression is undesirable: it suits neither our interests nor those of our people at home. Give facts by all means, but guard against indiscriminate enthusiasm that might cause imaginative persons to get the wrong idea.

Success

All new prisoners, still suffering from the trauma of their imprisonment plus whatever wounds they sustained in being shot down, were highly suspicious of the regulars in charge of the reception centre at Dulag Luft. The thinking was that anyone who had been given a job by the Germans must at least have some German sympathies, that someone given preferential treatment by the Germans must be giving something in return. There was also the Kriegie feeling – funny how quickly it could be incubated – of jealousy: that privileges could only be rackets, and therefore obnoxious. So it was that in March 1943 a jeering, booing and at the same time happy mob of Kriegies was to be seen in one corner of the compound. Our issue of March 4, carried the story, Old Dulagian Plies Pump.

> Cesspools and latrines are not generally a customary centre of attraction for humans – apart from Sanitary Inspectors – and it was with no little surprise that we noted a knot of sightseers around the wash-house of 42 and 46 blocks on Tuesday afternoon. Investigation proved that the spectacle providing so much interest was no less a person than an ex-Dulag Luft Permanent Staff Sergeant plying the cesspit pump. Many will recall Sgt. Eric Galloway from their short sojourn at Dulag and will wonder at this transition from the amenities of Frankfurt to the excrescence of Sagan.
>
> **Dropped in the mire**
> From the pumper's imprecations, muttered through a cloud of smoke, we gather he was the victim of a foul plot which was enacted at a recent *Appell* and from the attitude and remarks of the 44 block spectators, it was apparent that they were undisguisedly enjoying the sight of a formerly comfortable resident of Dulag undergoing the indignities of a pukkha prison camp.
> Galloway, we are told, took his punishment in a sporting manner and has not yet taken reprisals.
> No ill effect resulted from his arbeit and rumours of the odours affecting his appetite are without foundation.

The following day we carried an open letter from Sgt. G. Salmon, complaining about our report which had certainly become a camp talking point.

OPEN LETTER

Sir, Hitherto I have read the *Daily Recco* with interest and pleasure, but this morning I was grieved to find your newspaper debasing itself. I refer to the article on Mr Galloway's débacle. Such an incident is too common to need comment and the tone of the report is all too clearly an attack upon a personality. I am not an intimate friend of Mr Galloway, neither am I in any way concerned in past events but I do know that he has borne similar attacks like a gentleman and you yourself refer to his sportsmanship. Your newspaper does not rely on sales, neither has it competitors, and therefore your responsibility to your public is greater and in this I submit, you are failing if you permit the newspaper to become the medium of a private quarrel. I feel sure gentlemen, that your professional training must rebel against the idea of your brainchild becoming a tongue-pointing, mudslinging schoolboy. I am aware that the tone of this letter is stiff, but you are entitled to know that some of us will strongly oppose a descent into yellow journalism.

Yours etc, G.T. Salmon.

[Ed: We must disagree with the writer that this article was a personal attack on Mr Galloway. It was an unbiased report of a camp happening and rather than running him down, we appreciated his sportsmanship. We are in full agreement as regards yellow journalism and will endeavour, as before, to maintain our already good name which our readers have given us.]

The duress and restriction of prison camp life were bad enough, but to have a closed society within our society within the all-enclosing barbed wire was too much . . . that was at the root of the trouble which was sapping morale in the first few months of 1943.

The camp, now many hundreds strong, was run on the prisoners' side by a mess committee comprising representatives from each barrack block. Under the mess committee were smaller committees looking after particular aspects of camp life. In practice the entertainments committee, which had the difficult task of allocating time and space in the entertainment block for the many organisations clamouring for facilities, seemed to be all powerful – and totally secretive. It was the secretiveness of the entertainments committee and the bitter feelings engendered throughout the whole camp by its cloak and dagger activities, which helped bring the *Recco* into being. And in our first issue our lead story won us many supporters by announcing that the E.C was to be investigated.

The diversity of issues that interested Kriegies are shown on the next pages

[Continued on page 38]

OPEN LETTER

Dear Sir,

Considerable alarm is felt at the practice of spreading night soil on garden plots. While some ignorance regarding its possibilities may be condoned, surely those responsible must find difficulty in reconciling their actions with the points so frequently raised by the Group-Captain with the Commandant and the Red Cross.

The S.B.O. has repeatedly complained of the inadequacy of sanitation and, on occasion, protested against the depositing of excreta in the Vorlager. Yet, at N.C.O's requests, cargoes of filth have been spread within feet of certain Barracks.

In civilized countries the practice is heavily punishable: the prohibition arises not from purely olfactory reasons, but because of a very real and ever-present danger of infection. Do our misguided gardeners realize the Carnegie Institute has spent millions on the prevention of soil pollution?

I trust, Sir, that the sane majority will prevent the possibility of further risks in this respect.

Yours etc
J. Garrell.

OLD "DULAGIAN" PLIES PUMP!!

Cesspools and latrines are not generally a customary centre of attraction for humans - apart from Sanitary Inspectors - and it was with no little surprise that we noted a kno of sightseers around the washhouse of 42 and Blocks on Tuesday afternoon. Investigation prov that the spectacle providing so much interest no less a person than an ex-Dulag Luft per manent staff sergeant, plying the cesspit pu

Many will recall Sgt. Eric Galloway from their short sojourn at Dulag and will wonder at this transition from the amenities of Frankfurt to the excrescence of Sagan.

DROPPED IN THE MIRE?

From the pumper's imprecations, muttered through clouds of smoke, we gather he was the victim of a foul plot which was enacted at a recent Appel,

and from the attitude and remarks of the 4 Block spectators, it w apparent that they we undisguisedly enjoying sight of a formerly co fortable resident of Du undergoing the indign of a pukka prison ca Galloway, we are told took his punishment a sporting manner a has not yet taken repri no ill effects resulted f his arbeit, and rumours odour effecting his appeti are without foundation

INTRODUCING "C

RECCO

...STMAS

THURSDAY. 4ᵗʰ MARCH. 1943.

...OM OUR MAIL BAG

...Hannah V.C. has received ... discharge ··

An apple grower tells ... that in getting repairs ...e to the back axle of ...tractor, a case of ...sert apples saved him ...ks of delay ·· Two eggs, ...farmer assured me, en-...led him to get his ...tch seen to and today ...single egg tempted a ...chanic to work overtime··

In Covent Garden the ...y fruit that changed ...nds were grapes sold at ...a grape ...

...ED CROSS

A party went to the ...tion this morning at ...30 hours for personals.

PLAY THE GAME!

There were only 9 new foot-...s in the Store. Two were ...ed at the beginning of the ...k. One has not been seen ...ce. The other was found, ... lace and bladder having ...n removed!

ENTERTAINMENT

Sir,

I wonder how many of "For the love of Mike" play-goers thought, as I said, that the settee and armchairs were hired props instead of a super-product of the props people?

Yours etc,
"Staggered."

[ED. The settee and armchairs were designed by John Murrell, fashioned by "Wimpy" Wooton and "Foo" Fotheringham and covered by Maurice Cowley—Nice work boys!]

Matinees of the show will be held for the officers this after-noon and tomorrow afternoon at 13·00 hours. Note that the whole of 45 Block is out of bounds while the officers are over.

Seats 16 to 22 of row 5 have been removed, holders of these tickets for tonight will sit on top row.

The "Cooler" is at present full up, the overflow being accommodated in the Guardroom.

939 letters came into the Compound yesterday.

RECORD MONTH

February was a record month for book parcels, approx. 3413 books being censored. The previous best month was Jan-uary when 1816 books came in. Since September 1942 a total of 9988 books have come into the Compound.

Three windows were broken in the library last soccer season and have not been replaced. For the sake of the School and Library please re-frain from kicking footballs outside the building!

CAPTAIN VICTOR.

43 Bl. TO BEAT 55 Bl.
weather permitting.

RADIO

Yesterday's Report: Germans claim to have reached the middle Donetz in a broad front. In accordance with the policy of shortening the line, the town of Rochew was evacuated according to plan!!

WANTED

Pair of tennis shoes size 7 for pair size 9 (new).
McCurdy. 42 N.

WEATHER FORECAST

Bright intervals, occasional showers, cool wind.

YESTERDAYS WEATHER

MAX. 7·5°C
MIN. 3·5°C
RAINFALL NIL.

PRINTED AND PUBLISHED BY THE MACKAY BUTCHER PRESS

BIG EETZ"

CIGARETTE CHARITY SCHEME

INSURANCE BENEFIT

Sir,

A group of us has been discussing the possibility of launching a scheme to increase the weekly issue of cigarettes from 50 to 100 for "hard-up members of this compound."

If you would grant me an interview I feel sure I could put before you some practicable ideas.

Voluntary support by the wealthier members of this compound is a necessity, and I suggest an appeal for this might be made through the medium of the "Daily Recco".

Yours etc
"Pro Bono Publichouse"

Re - the above letter the "Daily Recco" interviewed the sender and the scheme was outlined as follows.

If names of donors are forthcoming a committee would be set up to launch the scheme.

WEEKLY ISSUE

The members of this committee would be in touch with Block Leaders who would make out a list of those in their blocks willing to forego the whole, or part, of their Red X issue. Handed in to the Block Leaders also, would be the names of those who really depend on the weekly issue.

These names would then come before the Committee for investigation. The blocks chiefly concerned would be 39 and 40.

FOR HARD TIMES

The Committee would also be willing to run an insurance scheme against hard times. If at present you are comfortably off but have doubts as to the future, you simply pay a premium now. When your cigarette parcels slow up or stop, you are then able to draw benefit from your investments.

There are many cigarettes in the camp. Remember charity begins at home!

All interested please call in at our office.

GROUP-CAPTAIN PRUNE

The Group-Captain, having annihilated most of the ? in the Red Cross Store, ha? turned his attention to bi? things. The Commandant's chicken escaped within a ?uch of its life when it ? roached the Red X store ear? yesterday. This is not the ? engagement. It is belie?? that the Red X representat?? are in league with the ca? to bring about the destruc? of the chicken!

POTTED DOG

A panic was caused ? several blocks in the Nor? end of the Camp when te? jaw-bones and a suppos? claw, were found in the R? meat on Wednesday.

All exhibits were colle? and taken to an expert, w? verdict was that the jaw-? and teeth were definitely ? and the "claw" a tooth from? pig's upper jaw.

So die all rumours !!

PEN LETTER

,

Hitherto I have read the ly Recco" with interest pleasure, but this ning I was grieved to d your newspaper de- ing itself. I refer to the icle on Mr Galloway's ele. Such an incident too common to need ment, and the tone he report is all too ly an attack upon a sonality.

I am not an intimate nd of Mr Galloway's ther am I in any way erned in past events I do know that he has e similar attacks like en tleman, and you your- refer to his Sports- nship.

our newspaper does not on sales, neither has ompetitors, and there- your responsibility to public is greater and this, I submit, you are ng if you permit the spaper to become the dium of a private quard e sure, gentleman, that proffesonal training t rebel against the of your brain-child ming a tongue-pointing, x-slinging schoolboy.

I am aware that the tone of this letter is stiff, but you are entitled to know that some of us will strongly oppose a descent into Yellow Journalism.

Yours etc.
G. T. Salmon.

[ED. We must disagree with the writer that this article was a personal attack on Mr Galloway, it was an un- biased report of a Camp happening and rather than running him down, we appreciated his sportsman- ship. We are in full agree- ment as regards Yellow Journalism and will en- deavour as before, to maintain our already good name which our readers have given us]

RED CROSS

200 loose personals and 40 sacks were collected yes- terday. It is hoped to list these today.

A wagon of Argentine bulk food also arrived.

It is reported from a reliable source that the Commandant's dachshund has been missing for the past two days !!

"New York Times" says "the situation screams out for a spring offensive by the Allies".

872 letters came into the Compound Yesterday.

EDUCATION

All those engaged in the Motor Trade and are interested in talks on the subject, are asked to meet in Library on Monday 8th March. After afternoon Appel.

MOTOR CLUB

H. E. Smith will talk about Motor Cycling and Motor-Cycles in New Zealand. Today at 6 P.M.

SAILING CLUB

"Aussie" Lascelles will give a talk on "Cruising round the French Coast". Today at 7-30 P.M.

CAPTAIN VICTOR

Block 42 to beat Block 51.

WANTED

Cigarette case and snap album.
Sgt. P. Clayden 56 S.

Tennis shoes size 9 for pair size 9.
Mc Curdy 42. 18.

Pair slippers large 8 or 9 for small pair size 8 new. (leather preffered)
Charlesworth 52.

WEATHER FORECAST

Fair, with average temperature and cool easterly winds by day. Frost at night.

YESTERDAY'S WEATHER.

MAX. 6.0°C
MIN −7.0°C   Rainfall. Trace.

PRINTED AND PUBLISHED BY
THE MACKAY BUTCHER PRESS

[continued from page 33]

Deans Commission

F/Sgt. James' proposal that there be an election of 5 men not connected with entertainments to make an enquiry into the E.C and to make a report to the Mess Cttee was carried. The following were elected: Sgt. Deans, Sgt. Gordon, F/Sgt. James, W/O Snowdon and Sgt. Lascelles.

Eleven issues later we carried a letter to the editor complaining about the arbitrary methods employed by the E.C. when dealing with a request that boxing shows should be allowed in the theatre. In an editorial we wrote:

> The E.C. are the only Ctte in the camp who have not so far invited us to attend their meetings.
> This is regrettable in as much as the compound do not therefore get the E.C point of view reported to them – on Feb. 26 we wrote to the Chairman of this body asking for press privileges, but have to date received no reply.

In the Stop Press of the same issue, dated February 27, we carried an item timed at 01.00 hours:

> Since going to press we have been notified verbally that our letter to the E.C. will come before their consideration later today.

And in Monday's edition we carried the story in column 1:

> The press was present
> At Saturday's meeting of the Entertainment's Committee the Press were granted full facilities to report all E.C. meetings and were allotted a Permanent Pass for the theatre.

Victory was ours – and the camp's. Rumours and jealousies previously flourishing in the dark would now die off, killed by the glare of publicity and open government. Bill Butcher and I were delighted to have achieved so much in so short a time.

The sanctuary of the secretive Entertainments Committee had been breached (see Column 1)

DAILY RECCO

299 DAYS TO CHRISTMAS   **DUTY BLOCK 44.**   **MONDAY, 1ST MARCH, 1943.**   ISSUE No. 13.

THE "CREAM" FLIES HOME!

FROM OUR MAIL BAG.

...The papers yesterday said the Royal Air Force prisoners are to be flown home...

...Rommel's on the run...would a recuperating Kriegie like a reservation made at a holiday centre? Say for mid-September? Would it be too optimistic, I wonder? It might be worth a 5/- bet, anyway...

...If cigarette parcels are not being received by P.S.O.W. the next-of-kin can enquire at the firm of origin and they will receive express labels.

...Kay Francis, Carole Landis, Martha Raye, Mitzi Mayfair, Edward G. Robinson have been here for two months and are

now going round the garrison towns entertaining the troops. They have all broadcast two or three times, and Carole Landis has married an American Captain of the Eagle Squadron.

...we are now allowed 20 coupons for each personal clothing parcel.

...In the papers that yours is the only Camp that could buy Xmas gifts and send them home.

TOC. H.

Re—our "Strike" article. Toc. H. claim that there is some misunderstanding. They state that they turned down this job on the principle that it was not a volunteer one and because pressure was being applied by the Germans.

CONTINUED.

Stage Manager and Sgt. Merril was appointed to his place.

Sgt. Bailey has also resigned from the Entertainments Committee.

CONDITION IMPROVING

Sgt. Joyce passed a fairly good day. His condition is not serious although he is weak from loss of blood.

RED X FOOD SCHEME

A new scheme for issuing Red X Food suggested by the officers was discussed by the Red X Food representatives yesterday afternoon...

NO DETAILS

Full details of the scheme are not yet available and it will not come into operation until the move to the New Officers Camp. The Camp Leader and the Secretary were present at the meeting.

N.C.O.'s PARTY

The main point of the scheme is for the distribution of parcels to be done by a permanent working party from our Compound. This will include permanent office staff and a party for unloading at the station and work in the Vorlager. It is expected that 40 N.C.O.'s will be required for this work. The names of men chosen for this work is to be submitted to the Germans today.

MAIN DEPOT

The aim of the scheme appears to be to centralize distribution for the three Compounds. S/Ldr. Torrens will be Camp parcels officer.

At the moment the situation is vague as the Germans have yet to deal with the proposed scheme.

GERMANS "BELT"

Two Germans were seen yesterday afternoon thieving potatoes from a clamp on the west side of the camp. An Unter Offizier took them in charge!!

ROLL-UP!!

"Honest" Winnie Stalag's premier turf accountant will oblige patrons by "laying the odds" on all 1st division football and rugby matches. (betting in cigarettes. min 10.)

WANTED.

Copy of the play "Winterset" by Maxwell Anderson.
    Camp Office.

Two 2.H. Pencils. Urgent.
    T.S. Campion. 41.13.

A photograph album.
    Dent 42. A.

Shorthand Sec. Neat handwriter. Full time job for show production. Apply "Daily Recco".

Copies of "The man who came to dinner". Education Office.

BASKETBALL.

Americans 9 - Canadians 38.

WEATHER FORECAST

Cloudy at first. Fair periods after midday. Average Temperature

YESTERDAY'S WEATHER

MAX. 9.6°C
MIN. 0.2°C   RAINFALL. TRACE.

PRINTED AND PUBLISHED BY THE MACKAY BUTCHER PRESS

Splitters

Letters were a vital link with home. They boosted morale. They stemmed insanity. They were the stuff that nurtured dreams and memories. But they were also a two-edged sword as various issues of the *Recco* revealed. Without letters, individuals – and the camp – suffered. Moodiness was engendered and acrimony flourished. Envy was there too, when, on the days that mail was issued, some prisoners got no news from home.

Letters were such an important part of camp life that the *Recco* regularly printed whatever news was available about them – that so many bags had been delivered from the station; that they would be issued on such and such a day and so on. For, even if they ended up only half-size because of the blue pencilling and scissor work of censors in both Britain and Germany, they were still something to be treasured, read, reread and then read again.

MAIL
"Out of 40,000 letters that arrived on February 1, this compound has had 19,760."

"This coming week more recent mail will be censored."

"1,044 letters came into the compound yesterday."

"719 letters came into the compound yesterday."

"February was a record month for book parcels, approximately 3,413 books being censored. The previous best month was January when 1,816 books came in. Since September 1942 a total of 9,988 books have come into the compound."

"430 letters came into the compound on Saturday. The total for last week was 2,637."

Some letters carried passages of unconscious humour and after the publication of one or two examples brought to us by Kriegies willing to share their chuckles, the *Recco* carried a regular feature of mailbag briefs, using the German term of *Splitter* from the Splitters or Briefs in the *Volkischer Beobachter* which along with the *Frankfurter Algemeine Zeitung* circulated in the camp. Thanks to Kriegies who could both speak and read German fluently these two newspapers formed a considerable part of our information on the progress of the War – albeit from a German propagandist point of view.

The extracts from our mates' mail amused and entertained and also, on occasion, informed – giving us the price of cinema tickets, beer, fags and so on. MB Splitters became a popular part of the paper and, from time to time carried Dear Johns. These were frequently harrowing letters from former lovers, girlfriends and wives who had found the loneliness of separation too much and who had sought – and found – solace in another's arms.

... the black georgette is still waiting for you.

... I have just recovered from an attack of influenza, so am at last able to write to you. (First letter from the writer for three years)

... it will be a wonderful education to be among the Germans for so long. They are a clever and interesting people ...

... Darling, if you tell me once more that you have had all your hair shaved off, I'll retaliate by doing the same and you wouldn't like to come home to a lot of stiff bristles, would you? ...

... Darling, don't keep saying you look 45. Anyhow I'll soon make you feel youthful again ...

... I've just been reading in the paper (so it is not secret now) that we are making jet-propelled planes, they fly at tremendous speed without a propeller. The inventor is G/C Frank Whittle. The paper also tells us that the Germans are producing hundreds of little pilotless bombers to bomb us. They say they can be catapulted from the ground and steered by radio ...

... You remember ___ who married a Pole? Well, she has just had a baby. She said to her Polish husband that she would like the baby to be called Sandy. Her husband said he didn't care if it was called Sandy, Monday or Tuesday ...

... Please let me know the thing you fancy most when you return. (from a mother)

... Mrs. Taylor, the insurance man's wife from across the road, has given you half a pound of chocolate. Her brother was repatriated and said he didn't need it ...

... Is it really true that you have a swimming pool there because we have heard so? ...

... Darling, in your letters you must not say that after the War you'll put yourself out to stud – it isn't nice ...

... Miss ___ has just had another baby. I don't know what the place is coming to ...

... Dear old chap, I am on my honeymoon, so as one captive to another ...

... I've tried so hard to get into the fighting forces – but as I'm under contract with my firm it's quite impossible – but it's fellows like you who make men like me envious ...

... I can't send you a food parcel without a label, which according to the local POW magazine you can get easily from the German government, so do try and get one.

... Darling, when you write, tell me more about your camp. Do you do any horse-riding or similar activities? ...

... Well pal, I must say cheerio now, see you again in about a year's time ...

... We had a pre-war Christmas, plenty of toys and plenty to eat, two large trees and a party with jellies and blancmange, mince-pies and a turkey ...

... A towel costs 12/11 if you can get one, but you can get one for 2/11 from the POW Relatives Association ...

... My dear son, I am sending you a postal order so that you can buy some chocolate ...

From an A.T.S. girl: ... I had to go on dental parade the other day and I was naturally quite scared. But the dentist and I made a date so I'm not scared any more ...

Most Dear John recipients hid their grief, some purged their souls with profanity, some in bravado and others, possibly wreaking a sort of vengeance, brought them to be published. The general consensus among the men whose magnetism had lasted only as long as they were there in the flesh, was that it was inevitable that their girlfriend/wife should accept the advances of someone else in the Forces – even a Yank. What was beyond bearing was the thought that some civilian in a cushy, safe, well-paid job should be the usurper of the female's affections.

While letters from home were worth their weight in gold, Kriegies were sometimes guilty of not realising that their letters to Blighty were just as welcome. Sometimes the *Recco* had to remind the camp that letters home had to be submitted for censorship before a certain date. Each prisoner was allowed two letters – folded, four inch wide strips capable of carrying about 500 words in small script – and four postcards a month.

Many heart-searching decisions had to be made about whose turn it was to receive a letter or a postcard; which member of the family should receive which, and what, at the end of the day, to write anyway when one day was much the same as another – only worse. One Kriegie solved the problem by using one of his postcards to carry nothing but the simple message – Read Hebrews Chapter 13, Verse 8. The recipient, looking up the Good Book at the appropriate passage, was enlightened, if not heartened, by the phrase, "Jesus Christ the same yesterday, and today and for ever."

Many prisoners used their mail home to pass on coded messages which met with varying degrees of success. Some of the codes were concocted by the prisoners and their mates/families while they were still free men; some, devised by prisoners, without prior knowledge by their folks back home, caused only wrinkled brows and comments about the poor lad's mental state as puzzled relatives pondered the significance of lions roaring in obscure German villages which, seemingly, were prone to have eagles flying overhead. But, throughout the camp grapevine, we learned of messages that had gone home and been understood and of replies printed on food wrappers in Red Cross parcels, with the connivance of the Air Force and ignorance of the Geneva-based Red Cross Organisation. There were too a number of individuals who sent and received coded messages – officially – through the whole period of their captivity.

It was an amazing and encouraging feature of camp life that old Kriegies could, in passing on extracts from their letters to the *Daily Recco*, laugh at themselves and allow the rest of the camp to laugh as well. These examples taken at random from the revived *Recco* are still amusing all these years later.

Competition

Encouraged by the success of the *Recco*, Ron Mogg, a fellow prisoner who had been a journalist in civvy street before joining up – and being shot down – decided to run a rival Sunday newspaper entitled the *Weekly Brief*. Perhaps the decision to restrict his efforts to one day a week was made because on the nights the lark was singing, he took down in shorthand the British news bulletins picked up on Curly Bristow's home-made and illicit radio. But, in addition to opting for a once a week journal, Ron also decided to titillate his readers with camp gossip . . . revealing, on occasion, romances between prisoners.

It was a fact of camp life that some prisoners were attracted to each other and were repelled by others. In the main, relationships between Wingers, as close companions were known, were completely platonic. Despite the sudden, in most cases literally overnight, loss of normal sexual relationships with girls, wives and lovers back home in Blighty, most prisoners gave up sex for the duration . . . without any conscious thought or ill-effect. But it must be admitted that there were isolated cases where friendship took on, in most cases gradually, a physical as well as mental dimension. Provided the participants kept it to themselves and did their best to hide it, their barrack-room mates ignored it.

Specially susceptible to sudden advances of friendship were the prisoners who played female parts in the camp plays and revues. Generally, the stage-door Johnny who went round to the female's barrack in a hot flush of passion and then saw him in the cold light of day surrounded by the trappings of an ordinary Prisoner of War, quickly lost his enthusiasm. The girl, pleased to be praised over her stage performance, was generally quick to point out, 'Watch it mate – it was only an act.'

The *Weekly Brief* made snide references to certain Wingers and friendships. This prompted a bitter editorial from the *Recco* in its issue of March 16:

Decency Outraged
There appears to be some doubt in the camp, as to whether or not the *Daily Recco* and the *Weekly Brief* are associated newspapers. They are not and what is

more, the *Daily Recco* wishes publicly to disassociate itself from the appalling standard of sensational journalism that has been set in the first two issues of the Sunday paper.

False News

To justify the denouncement, we must point out that the *Weekly Brief* has already published false news: it has elaborated upon rumours instead of squashing them: it has published an unfair report of a public meeting and it is outraging all accepted canons of decency.

With regard to the last accusation we would prefer to believe that the compound does not consist largely of sexual perverts. Consequently the many scurrilous innuendoes published concerning the innocent practice of winging constitute a deliberate insult to the compound as a whole.

Honesty to Public

In conclusion, we would refer the editors of the *Weekly Brief* to the advice given by the Daddy of all journalists, Mr F.J. Mansfield (20 years editor of *The Times* and a former President of the National Union of Journalists) who said If a journalist is to gain honour in his own country he must treat his public honestly and fairly.

The following month we carried a reader's letter echoing our sentiments:

Sir, Yesterday I went to read the *Weekly Brief* hoping to find after the public denunciation of the proprietors on Saturday (when a mock trial was held) that the standard of this rag had been improved.

I was disgusted however to see that this perpetration of filth had reached an even lower level.

Many people here are studying, and find it hard to obtain the necessary paper. The paper that is being wasted on the *Weekly Brief* could surely be put to better use by the above-mentioned student Yours etc, R. Ayre.

Shortly after that the *Weekly Brief* died . . . its passing unmourned. It was this weekend gap that Australian Dennis Adams tried to fill later on when he left the *Recco* . . . but his venture too, while not following the *Weekly Brief's* salacious line, did not last for more than a few issues.

Parcels Up

Parcels up. The cry echoed round the camp, bouncing off barrack blocks, breaking up bridge games, stopping studies and even interrupting arguments. Eager hands followed by eager bodies raced to help unload the carts bearing the precious Red Cross parcels.

The race to help and speed up the delivery into each block was not activated by gluttony – although there was some of that in it too – it was not caused by curiosity, but simply that the distribution was a welcome break in the camp routine and monotony. Every Prisoner of War worth his Klim knew exactly what was in each different type of parcel. With eyes closed he could reel off the type of biscuits, meat loaf (one Scottish variety was more loaf that meat), bully, chocolate, soap, sardines, pilchards, stew, spam, tinned rice or whatever, that was contained in each parcel. And he could assess, to within five minutes on any particular day, just how long the parcel would last. Combines of men would have their menus planned to cope with British, Canadian or American parcels and the slight variations of provisions within each type.

A combine was a group of like-minded Kriegies who decided to 'mess' together, sharing the contents of their Red Cross parcels (except the chocolate!) with each person taking his turn to cook. Like most other prisoners our crew formed a combine and, like most other prisoners, one or two drifted off over the months, to form other combines with 'townies' or like-minded souls, or even, in extreme cases, to operate in a combine of one.

The only time when forward planning gave way to the harsh reality of immediacy was when parcels were scarce and instead of one parcel per man the issue was restricted to one parcel between six or eight. On those occasions experience taught us that the best way to share out was to put all the unsweets together in a stew and all the sweets into a glop which, according to the ingredients, could be titillating or merely yugh!

One type of biscuit, like old ship's hardtack, was extremely popular. Soaked in water it grew to at least double the size. With some of the water then squeezed out, the biscuit was fried – the filling effect was significantly increased. Another favourite was the Canadian dried milk which went under the trade name of Klim. It took some backward prisoners some time to work out that Klim was milk spelt backwards. But there was nothing backward about the product. It mixed without leaving lumps, it could be made thick like cream and the tins, larger than the normal stew or fruit in syrup tin, made an ideal cooking utensil. I don't think there was a single combine in the camp which did not have a Klim cook-pot, Klim drinking mug or Klim something or other in their possession. Parts of Klim tins were basic ingredients in the clock made by Bernard Channing. The clock, like the milk, was smooth – the Kriegie accolade for anything excellent.

At different camps physical characteristics of the buildings and the number of prisoners contained behind the barbed wire, regulated the method of cooking and consequently the distribution of Red Cross parcel contents. In some camps cooking was done on an individual or combine basis with the cookhouse supplying only hot water (three times a day) and stews of watery veg, millet, barley etc, twice a day). In others all the meat and sweets from the parcels were taken to the cookhouse to be made into communal dishes, which, according to the cookhouse staff's ability were either good or barely edible. All but the laziest Kriegies preferred doing their own or combine thing. Especially after the discovery of the blower. This ingenious invention (built largely of Klim tins) produced, through a hand-driven fan, a blast of air under the firebox and guaranteed the maximum amount of heat from the minimum amount of fuel. And with wood always in extremely short supply, this was the ideal that everyone aimed at.

The Red Cross was a vital lifeline for all Kriegies. Without it the only prisoners to survive would have been those captured only a few weeks before the end of the war. For the rest of us the supplement brought to our meagre German-provided diet was vital. Even so, the prisoners who returned to the UK in the summer of 1945 were mere shadows of the men shot down years previously. My own skinny seven stones was the trigger for massive cooking sprees back home in Broughty – rationing or no rationing. But while the Red Cross supplies kept us alive, they also created some arguments. Prison camp life certainly brought out the best – and worst – in all of us. In issue No. 34 the *Recco* carried a leader on the question of invalid parcels – special parcels containing extra-nutritional foods.

Only a few hours after that issue was pinned up at the end of the barrack, we had an irate reader calling at our office (bed space) with a hastily scrawled personal response to our editorial. Naturally his reply was featured in the following day's issue – it saved us scrounging around for another lead article and proved that the paper was justifying its existence. Ironically the very same issue of the paper carried a letter from the prisoner in charge of the issue of Red Cross parcels stating that because officers were

Black Bread Recipe

(For POW camps, taken from the official records of the Food Providing Ministry in Berlin, dated 24/5/41)

50%	Bruised rye grain
20%	Tree flour (ie sawdust)
20%	Sliced sugar beet
10%	Minced leaves & straw

Rations of bread bulked up with sawdust, leaves and straw explained some of the weight loss by prisoners

moving into a new compound at the camp, it was likely that German personnel involved in parcels issues would be fully occupied searching the officers during the change-over, and that there would, consequently, be no issue of ordinary food parcels that week.

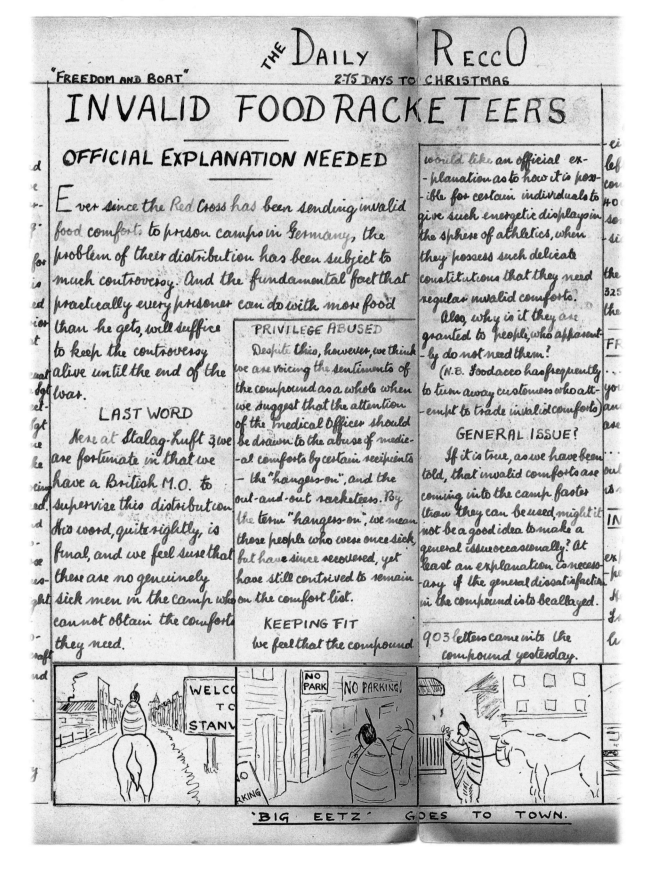

THE DAILY RECCO

"FREEDOM AND BOAT"   2·75 DAYS TO CHRISTMAS

INVALID FOOD RACKETEERS

OFFICIAL EXPLANATION NEEDED

Ever since the Red Cross has been sending invalid food comforts to prison camps in Germany, the problem of their distribution has been subject to much controversy. And the fundamental fact that practically every prisoner can do with more food than he gets, will suffice to keep the controversy alive until the end of the war.

LAST WORD

Here at Stalag-Luft 3 we are fortunate in that we have a British M.O. to supervise this distribution. His word, quite rightly, is final, and we feel sure that there are no genuinely sick men in the camp who cannot obtain the comforts they need.

PRIVILEGE ABUSED

Despite this, however, we think we are voicing the sentiments of the compound as a whole when we suggest that the attention of the medical officer should be drawn to the abuse of medical comforts by certain recipients – the "hangers-on", and the out-and-out racketeers. By the term "hangers-on", we mean those people who were once sick, but have since recovered, yet have still contrived to remain on the comfort list.

KEEPING FIT

We feel that the compound would like an official explanation as to how it is possible for certain individuals to give such energetic displays in the sphere of athletics, when they possess such delicate constitutions that they need regular invalid comforts?

Also, why is it they are granted to people who apparently do not need them?

(N.B. Foodacco has frequently to turn away customers who attempt to trade invalid comforts)

GENERAL ISSUE?

If it is true, as we have been told, that invalid comforts are coming into the camp faster than they can be used, might it not be a good idea to make a general issue occasionally? At least an explanation is necessary if the general dissatisfaction in the compound is to be allayed.

903 letters came into the compound yesterday.

'BIG EETZ' GOES TO TOWN.

LETTER TO THE EDITOR

FOOD QUEUE MEMBER HITS BACK

Sir,

As a recipient of invalid food since last Tuesday, and as one who exercises before morning parade, may I bring to your attention several aspects of the "food racketeering" question which you may not have considered.

Extra food is divided into two classes. Building up diet, and special diet, ie. gastric and similar cases where one is unable to digest ordinary rations. I can only speak from experience of the first class. An N.C.O. placed on this diet is thoroughly examined by the M.O. who, if he considers that the patient is undernourished or has suffered loss of weight through illness, or other causes such as "arrestlok", orders him to report on the extra food parade. In cases where there is loss of appetite it is often necessary to take sufficient exercise to restore his appetite. He is then able to cope with the unappetising "Reich" rations and the more nourishing supplementary diet.

The diet is discontinued when either the M.O. considers the patient is returned to normal, or if he himself asks to be removed from the list.

I am not suggesting that this privilege is never abused. I agree that an investigation would be an excellent thing. However I think you might have interviewed those in receipt of extra food and heard their story, before writing an article which tends to discredit all those who receive food and who also exercise.

Your paper can and has done a tremendous amount of good in the Compound. I hope you will continue to expose rackets, but not get the average "Kriegie" outlook which considers everything a racket which does not immediately benefit him.

Yours etc.
W. Harrison.

[Ed.. We investigated this matter thoroughly and found that certain Combines, when short of milk, send one of their number across for an extra ration.

404 letters came into the Compound yesterday.

FROM OUR MAIL BAG

15th Feb. ... We hear that the Germans will not guarantee air transport from Lisbon unless the mail is cut down...

... About mid-summer I shall send your skates for next winter ... This will be a bitter struggle until the end ... it will last a long time yet.

.. I was reading the P.O.W. leaflet yesterday and I see that you get a regular issue of cod liver oil and malt ... Do you take yours?

.. I didn't get any satisfaction from the Red Cross concerning your personal parcel which they returned to me after keeping it 3 months .. the only apparent reason for them holding it up and returning same, was because I wrote and told them I might be changing address shortly and would notify them if I did so ..

... You will probably be pleased to know that the regulations issued last week re letter-cards only being sent by air has been superceded by a further announcement ... all correspondence will be sent by air now.

Restrictions

At the beginning of April 1943 morale in the camp was rising, helped no doubt by the war news we were receiving that things were not going well for the Germans on the Russian front.

But while our morale was on the up, relations with the Kommandantur and the German guards were deteriorating. Reprisals were the order of the day although at Sagan things were not as bad with us as we believed them to be with other Allied prisoners in other camps. In our issue of April 12 we reported:

Schubin Surrounded by Mines
From Schubin comes the report of super-safety precautions taken by the Germans. After a big break by officers and men, the authorities laid land mines around the camp and put up additional wire 50 yards away from the main one. The area between was floodlit by searchlights.
Dynamite was used to blow tunnels in and in certain cases Russians were used to dig up tunnels.
One NCO working on a bread-loading party at the station succeeded in escaping taking with him a loaf from the lorry.
When the party first reached Schubin from this camp five months ago, they had 3 roll-calls in the morning and 3 in the afternoon. This was later altered to 2 in the morning and 3 in the afternoon.

Two days later we annoyed the Germans by painting the other side of the picture – relating an account, culled from a new Canadian airman, of how cushy life was for German prisoners in the hands of the Allies. The fact that the details dealt with events in 1940 and that conditions might have changed since then, did not make the reaction of our fellow Kriegies, or the German guards, any easier.

One of the new Kriegies – an ex-guard at a German POW camp in Canada – in an interview yesterday provided the following details of prison life in British hands.
The German prisoners are given the same rations as the Canadian army, receiving fresh milk, white bread, butter and eggs.

They have a daily meat ration and occasionally eat bacon for breakfast. The men, who were mostly merchant seamen, were billeted in an old fort.

There were 12 men in a room and they slept on beds with springs and mattresses. Each man had four blankets. Every Saturday the prisoners held a sale of articles which they had made. The Camp Captain fixed prices and the guards were allowed to buy models for souvenirs. These models were bought with Canadian currency with which the men could then buy chocolate, cigarettes and pop in their canteen. The prisoners also had a regular issue of bottled beer. There was no limit to the length of letters written to Germany. The local YMCA and other organisations gave concerts with women in the casts. Women were later banned however as the prisoners abused the privilege.

The Germans, who were very keen on football and basketball, also had frequent track events, the winners of which were given a special cake by their comrades. In the summer they were taken to a nearby lake to swim. Tennis courts were also provided.

One of the prisoners smuggled himself into a piano which left the camp to go into stores. Some considerable time later the warehouse watchman discovered him firmly wedged inside the piano and unable to move.

On the way over to Canada an attempt was made by the Germans to capture their transport. The attempt was foiled, two Germans being wounded in the process.

Ed: These extracts deal with one of the first POW camps formed in Canada in 1940.

On April 16, 1943 we reported extracts of a speech made in Essen by Hitler's Propaganda Minister Dr. Goebbels. Our article ended with Goebbels comment, "The English are in no way materially but only temporarily, psychologically, in a better situation – our inhabitants have much to suffer yet . . . they can inflict on us considerable damage."

The *Recco* of the following day reported British bombing of the Ruhr and Stuttgart, the retreat of the German Army in Tunisia and the confident forecast that should Rommel try to evacuate North Africa it would be worse than Dunkirk.

Morale in the camp was high and we reflected it in the columns of the *Recco*, taking care, nonetheless, never to print any of the news spread through the camp by couriers who had been given details of the British war news reported on the BBC and picked up by Curly Bristow's radio. But our articles were showing more and more anti-German feeling and on April 21 we carried the story of the Katyn massacre.

Alleged Russian Atrocities at Katyn
From Stockholm comes the news that the German press has accused the Soviets of murdering 12,000 Polish Officers in the Forest of Katyn near Smolensk.

The Polish Government in England has requested the International Red Cross to undertake an investigation into the matter.

It is asserted that in September 1939, 181,000 Polish Officers and men became Russian Prisoners of War. These were assigned partly to three camps: 4,500 to Kozielsk east of Smolensk; 3,920 Officers to Stara Bjelsk near Charkow and a further 6,750 to Ostasszhivo near Kalinin.

After the Polish-Soviet agreement of July 1941 some Polish Prisoners of War were set free, but not one from the above mentioned camps.

Reuter reports that this story is probably German propaganda and Moscow has announced that the graves at Katyn are merely archaeological excavations. From America and England comes the information that the skeletons are relics of the Stone Age, which the Germans have dressed in Polish uniforms.

Our German readers, and we knew we had them, could not have been amused by the tone the *Recco* was taking. We knew that time was running out. That the idea of a free press – even behind barbed wire – was something that could not long be tolerated. But the following day we continued the baiting of our German captors with a call to give full support to Dixie Deans in his 'Private War' with the Kommandantur.

Deans Completes Year as Leader

The Barth contingent came into this camp one year ago today. Congratulations to Sgt. Deans who has been Camp Leader since our arrival and who has had a very hard and delicate job to carry out.

United Front

At the present moment he is in disgrace and at 'war' with the German authorities. It is the compound's duty to back Sgt. Deans up and show the Germans that the Camp Leader has our full cooperation.

The Gen

Dixie was born on 25th January, 1914, is married and has no family. In 1936 he joined the RAF as a direct entry. Was shot down on 10th Sept 1940. Baled out and the kite just missed a customs house on the Dutch frontier.

He spent two holidays in Germany in 1937 and '38.

In his own words he is flat out for the mob – "I know an easy job when I see one."

A few days later, on Tuesday April 27, we devoted over half the *Recco* to reports of Japanese reprisals on American aircrew who had bombed Tokyo and other Japanese cities. Our article said that the German's Japanese allies had sentenced to death a number of the airmen whom they claimed had killed civilians and children and had not acted honourably – in the Japanese fashion. The article required no editorial from us and every Kriegie in the camp knew why we had printed it . . . so did our German guards.

The writing on the wall was soon to come off it. And on May 4, in issue no. 65 of the now lusty, thriving newspaper that had first appeared on February 15, the *Recco* said:

News Restrictions Spell Finish

It is with real regret that the editors of the *Daily Recco* have this morning to tell their readers that this will be our last issue unless the Germans will consent to raise certain bans on our sources of news.

At the conference with the Kommandant yesterday Sgt. Deans was informed that a camp newspaper would be tolerated only on the following conditions: 1. No political stories must be published; 2. The sheet would contain no war news; 3. Camp politics (i.e. relations with the Germans) are forbidden; 4. Before publication the paper is to be censored by a German officer.

Under these conditions we know from experience that it would be impossible to produce a daily newspaper of any sustained interest. The three news sources banned represent at frequent periods 75% of our copy.

We can only hope that if the authorities will condescend to peruse our previous 63 issues which have apparently given no cause for complaint, they will see their way clear to allow us to continue as before.

And in another article in the same issue we paid our tribute – along with our thanks – to Dixie Deans for the support he had given us in this unique enterprise which had helped to improve the quality of life for some of our fellows – and for us the editors as well.

Bill Butcher and I settled down to a private holiday in our holiday camp – the one the folks back home thought had a swimming pool, dance band, beer hall and everything except dancing girls. Like the cartoon of Big Eetz in the last issue, we rode off into the sunset.

The *Daily Recco's* **coverage of developments in the war and of Camp Leader Dixie Deans' conflict with the camp authorities led to its banning by the Germans. The sequence of issues in the run-up to this are reproduced on the following pages**

KEEP IT CLEAN

The best indication of the high standard of morale in Stalag Luft 3, is to be found in the ever-increasing interest taken in sport. It is affording the best possible exercise for the players, and, what is equally important, it acts as a great incentive as a spectacle in getting hundreds of other men out of the stuffy atmosphere of the barracks, into the open air.

This increasing interest is probably the main reason for the greater keenness with which games are being played this year. It is definitely to be encouraged, for it makes for better football and better spectacle.

There is, unfortunately, one great drawback to this competitive keenness – that is, that certain individuals are finding in it, an excuse to introduce into our soccer games, many of the more doubtful touches that marred professional football in pre-war England.

Such incidents as outbursts of temper, arguing with the referee, appealing to the crowd, and the deplorable professional habit practised by some teams of shaking hands all round after a goal, are absolutely unnecessary and they are putting the clock back as far as good sportsmanship is concerned.

Any "Kriegie" who remembers the fine displays of the famous Corinthians in England, will wonder why the spirit of soccer in the Camp has fallen below the standard set by those great amateurs.

We are all amateurs here, and we all play for the pure fun of the game. So let us try in our small way to put the great game of soccer back on the pedestal it occupied before such things as match bonuses and high transfer fees were ever thought of.

IN AND AROUND

52 new N.C.O's are expected to arrive today. This will mean extra beds in all barracks.

It is reported that the tools will be returned to the Theatre today.

770 letters came into the Compound on Saturday.

SCHUBIN SURF

From Schubin co precautions taken by b by Officers and men, around the Camp and 50 yards away from th tween was floodlit b was used to blow tu Russians were made

One N.C.O. workin at the station, succe with him a loaf from

When the party f this Camp five months in the morning and was later altered to the afternoon.

FROM OUR MAIL BAG

... we were at the adero last week and B

chose the table and th best waiter for our party when you come back ...

... A Mother has five son four of which are servin

NDED BY MINES

the report of super safety
ermans. After a big break
uthorities laid land mines
t up an additional wire
ain one. The area be-
archlights. Dynamite
in, and in certain cases
g up tunnels.

bread-loading party
in escaping, taking
e lorry!!

reached Schubin from
they had 3 roll-calls
the afternoon. This
the morning and 3 in

ne having been killed.
The fifth on coming of
ge, is officially excused
oining up...

... we are expecting
ou round to tea some-
ime towards the end
f 1946...

... Shortly we hope to
o down to check over the
a. and all our goods
nd chattels, as we shall
e wanting to get them
ut of their long storage
oon... [ED. This is from
usually pessimistic
ource]

ENTERTAINMENT

Last night's Classical
Concert presented by the
Musical Society, rose to
highest expectations and
marked a new phase in
Compound Entertainment.

A well chosen programme
- high musicianship and
fine team work character-
ised the whole production.
Frank Hunt was received
with loud applause and
Ned Herzstam once again
held the audience enrapt.
This concert marks the
first appearance of Frank
Hunt and "Curly" Herzstam
together, and their fine
team-work was much in
evidence. Polley, Charlesworth and Hart, contribute
handsomely to the enter-
tainment.

COMPETITION

Sgt. Hurst and Strick-
land and the person who
sent in the fisher girl story,
each receive 50 cigarettes
for last week's contest.

This week three copies
of "The Coloured Counties"
are to be given away as
prizes. They will go to the
persons who forecast most
nearly the number of books
which come into the Com-
pound through the Censor's
Office. Closing date is
Wednesday 14th April.

CAPTAIN VICTOR

46 Block to beat 44 Block
Brock, newly arrived from
Schubin, will play in goal
with Wright on the left
wing for 46 Block.

JAIL JOTTINGS

Sgt. H.J. Mason, sentenced
to 14 days for attempting to
escape from Dulag.

Sgt. S. Cawkwell, sentenced
to 14 days for attempting to
escape whilst on party unloading Schubin baggage.

WANTED

Wanted size 8 rubber shoes
in exchange for new pair
size 9.   Haynes. 39.

Wanted size 8 or 9 shoes
in exchange for size 7 new
shoes.   Pridham 56th

For Sale for cigarettes the following new books:-
Modern Plan Copying: Inter-
mediate Eng. drawing: Eng. and
workshop drawing: Foundations of
Tech. drawing: Applied Perspective:

WEATHER FORECAST

Further occasional rain
or showers at first. Some
bright periods later.

YESTERDAY'S WEATHER.

MAX. 50°F

MIN. 42°F   RAIN. ·11"

PRINTED AND PUBLISHED BY
THE MACKAY BUTCHER PRESS

96

FROM OUR MAIL BAG

... For the first time, England beat Wales at Wembley, by 5 goals to 3. Their Majesties attended the game. This match was Hapgood's 43rd appearance in international football and his 34th as Captain. It was a fast, keen game with Carter and Westcott scoring for England; Lowrie for Wales.

England: Marks: Bucuzzi, Hapgood: Britton, Cullis, Mercer: Matthews, Carter, Westcott, Hagan, Compton.

Wales: Poland: Turner, Hughes: Dearson, Jones, Powell: Hopkins, Lucas, Lowrie, B. Jones, Cummner.

... Have sent off your skates ready for next winter...

... Six bananas recently arrived in London, they were sold for £48...

... I had a letter from your Mother yesterday, she seemed quite amused, as you had written and asked her for your kid gloves and shoes; it rather disturbs me though, I have visions of you going off with a Fräulein...

ENTERTAINMENT

At yesterday's meeting of the E.C. it was decided that Band shows in future will be straight dance music recitals, with solos and vocals.

Starting after "Mikado" it is hoped to introduce a three-weekly cycle of shows. First week - stage show (A.D.S. or Variety); second week - recital (Theatre Orchestra or Dance Band); third week - Cinema.

There will be no more Sunday evening stage shows for the following reasons: One performance of each show would mean a too extravagant use of talent and material, whereas five performances of each could not necessarily be given on five consecutive Sunday evenings as the stage is very often not available immediately before a major show. Material would thus be tied up for six or even eight weeks, which could be used in major shows, which would depend on locally made costumes.

The period will be devoted to popular gramophone record recitals [E.D. The "Recco" Swing and Dance record programme, will take place this Sunday at 19.15 h.

Incidental music is required for "Home and Beauty". Anyone with recorded music of R. Forster, Gershwin, Ravel, R. Scott, Ellington, is requested to hand in the records to the "Recco" office. They will be returned on the same day.

Will the person who borrowed the record of "Slaughter on 5th Avenue" from Coles block 55, please return it immediately, as it is wanted for the above show.

If Charlie Hart and Jack James go to Barth, their places will be taken by Les Hall (piano) and Stan Parris (trumpet).

---

918 letters came into Compound yesterday.

RECCO
CHRISTMAS

ISSUE NO. 51.

WEDNESDAY. 14th APRIL. 1943

GERMANS' EASY LIFE IN CANADA

EX-GUARD'S STORY

One of the new "Kriegies" – an ex-guard at a German P.O.W. Camp in Canada – in an interview yesterday, provided the following details of prison life in British hands.

The German prisoners are given the same rations as the Canadian army, receiving fresh milk, white bread, butter and eggs. They have a daily meat ration and occasionally eat bacon for breakfast. The men, who were mostly merchant seamen, were billeted in an old fort. There were 12 men in a room and they slept on beds with springs and mattresses. Each man had four blankets.

Every Saturday the prisoners held a sale of articles which they had made. The Camp Captain fixed the prices and the guards were allowed to buy models for souvenirs. These models were bought with Canadian currency, with which the men could then buy chocolate, cigarettes and "pop" in their canteen. The prisoners also had a regular issue of bottled beer. There was no limit to the length of letters written to Germany.

The local Y.M.C.A. and other organisations gave concerts with women in the casts. Women were later banned, however, as the prisoners abused the privilege.

The Germans, who were very keen on football and basket ball also had frequent track events the winners of which were given a special cake by their comrades. In the summer they were taken to a nearby lake to swim. Tennis courts were also available.

One of the prisoners smuggled himself into a piano which left the camp to go into stores. Some considerable time later, the warehouse watchman discovered him firmly wedged inside the piano and unable to move.

On the way over to Canada, an attempt was made by the prisoners to capture the transport. The attempt was foiled, two Germans being wounded in the process.

[ED. – These extracts deal with one of the first P.O.W. Camps formed in Canada in 1940]

RED CROSS

1 wagon containing 1600 food parcels and 150 medical parcels and 1 wagon containing officers kit, arrived yesterday from Schubin. The second issue of food will possibly be on Friday as another party is expected from Schubin on Thursday.

Toothbrushes and toothpaste are urgently required for new arrivals. – Cpl. Little 46 N.

WEATHER FORECAST

Mainly fair, mild by day.

YESTERDAY'S WEATHER

MAX. 59°F

MIN. 40°F   RAIN. NIL.

CAPTAIN VICTOR – 52 to beat 51.

PRINTED AND PUBLISHED BY THE MACKAY BUTCHER PRESS

55

HEAD
OFFICE: BLOCK 42.N.
WIRE. MAC BUTCH.

"FREEDOM AND BOAT"

THE DAILY
254 DAYS

BRITISH AIR TERROR

GOEBBELS AT ESSEN

Dr Goebbels in a speech at Essen on the 10th April, moaned about the British terror raids and bombing of German culture. The depressing tone of the speech was offset by the news that the German U-Boats had England by the throat. He went on to say that the pressure was not yet felt, but would be later.

TIT FOR TAT

"It must always be remembered that the first bomb to be dropped on non-military targets was an English bomb— As all warnings were in vain and the British bombed our towns, then the German attacks on British territory began— They were from the beginning directed against military targets."

ATTACK ON MORALE

"The object of the bombing, as in the blockade of 1914-18, is to make the life of the German people hard to bear and break their spirit— It is self-evident that the air attacks which we have suffered,

(Lübeck, Rostock, Köln, Mainz, Essen and Antwerp are only a few examples named) —arise from a known plan which is the circle of the enemy's efforts and probably very far advanced"

CULTURE DESTROYED

"It makes the heart bleed to see the works of art and culture, known throughout the world, destroyed by the British air terror!"

"The English are in no way materially, but only temporarily, psychologically, in a better situation — Our inhabitants have much to suffer yet — they can inflict upon us considerable damage."

RALLY ROUND

The new arrivals are in urgent need of 20 tooth-brushes and toothpaste or powder. It has been suggested that the German powder issued recently would be suitable. Hand in to Cpl. Little 46. N.

MUSICAL SOCIETY

In future meetings this society for lecture recitals, will alternate to a normal gramophone recital on Sunday afternoon in the Theatre. An additional popular classical record recital will be presented monthly on Sunday evenings at 19.00 hrs.

There will be a meeting on Sunday next at 13.15 Full details later.

MOTOR SPORTS CLUB

Arthur Rutland will speak on "Electrical equipment of Motorcycles and cars" at tonight's meeting in the Library at 18.00 hours.

SAILING CLUB

At the society's meeting at 19.30 hours in the Library tonight, "Crash" Carter will lecture on "English Sailing types".

MAIL

Correct air-mail instructions should be placed on all letters for Colonies or Foreign Countries in the TOP LEFT-HAND CORNER. Instructions are posted in the Library lobby.

New arrivals are asked to remember to fill in the "Sender" portion of letters and cards. 523 letters came into the Compound yesterday.

SPORT

At yesterday's meet-
g of sports representat-
s in the Sports Store, it
as decided that a Com-
ound league knock-out,
ould take the place of
e present triangle com-
tition. All games are to
played on Sundays —
ch league running a
parate knock-out. Each
ague will play one game
ry Sunday. First matches
ill be played Sunday
e 18th.

Pitch-watering-blocks
e asked to do their
are.

No advance with cricket
rangements as Germans
e holding up string.

Anyone wanting to re-
air sports kit, will be
en full facilities in the
rts Store.

CAPTAIN VICTOR

Block to beat 42 Block

RED CROSS

Yesterday morning the
llowing arrived in the
p: 41 cases American par-
s (each case 16 parcels) =
6 parcels. 2 cases soap.
In the afternoon another
cases of American parcels
rived, containing 608 par-
s.

"WINNIE" SPEAKS

Winston Churchill, in
a speech given in March,
said that the war may
be finished this year or
next. He advised the
people, however, to pre-
pare for another 2 years
of war with Germany.
Further on in his speech,
the Prime Minister said
that the war with Japan
would probably go on for
2 years after the European
war and that complete
demobilisation etc. would
possibly come about in 4
or 5 years.

IN AND AROUND

Charlie Hart, yesterday
morning, after washing
his eiderdown, took out the
stuffing and laid it out in
the sun to dry. When dry
the quilt, on being rolled
up, started smouldering.
[ED. So all who wish to
take advantage of the hot
weather for washing and
drying their quilts, this is
a warning against the
dangers of spontaneous combustion.]

A German workman
came into the compound
yesterday wearing a green
felt hat. Whilst walking
around he was accosted
by a masked "bandit" who

ran away with his hat."!
Up to the time of going to
press the hat has not been
returned.

1350 seats were issued
on first day's booking
for "Home and Beauty."
The 3rd and 4th nights are
sold out. 13 seats are left
for 2nd night. 207 tickets
remain for 1st night and
the matinée has 370 left
out of 388. This is the
greatest number of seats
taken on the first day's
booking for any show.

WANTED

Wanted a new pair of
khaki shorts (waist 32")
in exchange for pair
(waist 36"). Thompson 553.

Wanted a reliable wrist
watch in exchange for
3000 cigarettes or chocolate.
Jarvis 425.

LOST on circuit yest-
erday, a small bone-hand-
led pen knife, cream coloured
Patch. 44.

WEATHER FORECAST

Continuing fine and warm
by day. Some high and
medium cloud.

YESTERDAY'S WEATHER

MAX 73°F
MIN. 43°F   RAIN. NIL.

104.

PRINTED AND PUBLISHED BY
THE MACKAY BUTCHER PRESS

HEAD
OFFICE: BLOCK 42N
WIRES. MAC BUTCH.
BY OBSERVER

"FREEDOM AND BOAT"

THE DAILY
253 DAY

WEEKLY WAR REVIEW

The thaw continues to hold up operations on the East front, and apart from Russian attacks N.W. of Izjum and on Kuban bridge heads, there is no further news of interest from the Russian front.

British bombing continues, the Ruhr and Stuttgart being the chief targets last week. Dr Goebbel's speech at Essen on the 10th of this month made quite clear the effects of the damage caused by bombing, and he made no attempt to minimise the seriousness of the situation, if it continued.

In Tunisia all last week the enemy have been falling back, and the area in which they are fighting continues to shrink.

It seems only a question of days now, before their total war-effort in Africa will be split up into localised fighting, as the British advance continues

If Rommel does make an effort to evacuate his African Corps, it will be worse than Dunkirk, and with that in mind, will probably fight till the last, although a number of his units will make some attempt to get away.

Before that happens however, I think that Rommel will make a stand and throw everything into it, inflicting the maximum amount of damage on us before he is beaten. If we are able to split his forces before he can do that, then the battle is almost over, and Germany loses one of its finest armies, both in men and material.

It is too much to expect the capture of Rommel, and in any case he has probably left Tunisia, a man of his experience, is far too valuable to Germany, to be left fighting in an action, which on the Eastern front would be described as "Cutting off the retreating army".

443 letters came into the Compound yesterday.

Yesterday afternoon 42 sacks and 107 loose personals were collected from the Station. The cigarette parcels have already been distributed.

There are now approximately 14,000 food parcels in store, enough for at least 4 weeks' issue. The present complement of the camp is 3,300 Officers and N.C....

THE G...

The undermentioned N.C.O. who wrote to have particulars of a "Dinghy dress is "Beehive works, Middlesex and Charlesway. The badge, as worn only on flying dress.

Another Club named the "Flying must have escaped ritory.

Dear Sir,

The Secretary of good enough to forward regard to the ditching. As this automatically the above Club, I enclose badge, which I hope you

We are issuing mem...

CHURCH

In the case of the Theatre being closed on Sunday, it is hoped to hold two open-air services.

These will be in the morning and evening at the usual hours.

"HOME AND BEAUTY"

Owing to the closing the Theatre, the above show will not take place as advertised. It will be ready within a few days of the Theatre re-opening.

GOLDFISH CLUB

A letter was received by an Caterpillar Club asking for the Goldfish Club's address, Bolpot lane, Stanmore, Robertson is the Hon. Secretary shown, may be clothing and battle—

has been started Boot Club. Members from occupied ter—

Caterpillar Club has been the particulars with which you were involved. as you as a member of with your membership

cards in addition to these badges, but unfortunately I am awaiting further supplies from the manufacturers. One of these cards should be forwarded to you within the course of a week or so.

I trust this correspondence will not cause you any inconvenience, but the Caterpillar Club assure me that they are in the habit of writing to prisoners of war.

Perhaps there may be other R.A.F. members in your camp who are eligible for this Club, if so, please give them my best wishes, and let them know I shall be pleased to hear from them

Yours etc.
C. A. Robertson.

CAPTAIN VICTOR

Block 46 to beat block 44

"C.C.C."

Within the last few days we have received numerous enquiries as to the meaning of "C.C.C." The initials stand for Civilian Conservation Corps — a nation-wide scheme started by Roosevelt in 1931.

The children of poorer families, after leaving school, were sent to work in lumber camps and were paid 25 dollars a week. 20 dollars of this money was sent home to their parents.

The youths were provided with clothing and kits of the same type as those which came into the camp on Wednesday.

When the scheme was inaugurated it was attached to the Army Corps. The public, however, fearing it to be a type of conscription, appealed and the C.C.C. was set up as a separate body.

IN AND AROUND

At the extra roll-call yesterday afternoon. Sgt. Barlow. 42.—was given 10 days hard for attempting to regain the ranks. Sgt. Willshaw. 42.— 14 days hard for nearly succeeding in regaining ranks and Sgt. McKenzie 44. was put straight inside for smoking.

Brodie 56. was taken to Sick-Bay yesterday, having broken his collar bone.

WANTED. A reliable wrist -watch. 3000 cigarettes or choc -olate.   JARVIS 42. 5.

WEATHER FORECAST

Anti-cyclonic conditions will prevail. Fair or fine with high temperatures by day. Cool at night.

YESTERDAY'S WEATHER.

MAX. 72°F
MIN. 46°F   RAIN. NIL

PRINTED AND PUBLISHED BY
THE MACKAY BUTCHER PRESS

FROM OUR MAIL BAG

... This is just a letter so that you shall know that we of the Red Cross in Derby, are so very glad that you are safe.. I am sure you will be interested to know that we came fourth in the country - and that includes London - in raising money. ... The children especially have helped — two little girls had a concert and sold their bracelets and beads, and yesterday brought me 18/6 - "nearly two parcels," they said. This you must think of as a very charming gift ... We have just opened a scheme here so that your relatives may buy from us anything they need for you, that they find difficult to get in the ordinary shops. We seem to have everything - including a most excellent pipe for 1/9. If anyone is unable to pay for the goods, they are still supplied. So with this scheme, which is now in operation all over the country, we hope that anything that any of you ask for will be sent to you ...

ALLEGED RUSSIAN ATROCITIE AT KATYN

From Stockholm comes the news that th German press has accused the Soviets of murderi 12000 Polish Officers in the forest of Katyn near Smolensk.

The Polish Government in England has quested the International Red Cross to underta an investigation into the matter.

It is asserted that in September 1939, 181,000 Polish Officers and men became Russi prisoners of war. These were assigned partly t three camps: 4500 to Kozielsk east of Smolensk 3,920 officers to Starabjelsk near Charkow, and a further 6,750 to Ostasszkoo near Kalinin.

After the Polish-Soviet agreement of July 19 some Polish prisoners of war were set free, but n one from the above mentioned camps.

Reuter reports that this story is probably Ger propaganda and Moscow has announced that graves at Katyn are merely archaeological excav ations.

From America and England comes the i formation that the skeletons are relics of the st -age, which the Germans have dressed in Polis uniforms.

RED CROSS

Three men went to the station this morning, on the usual routine visit, to collect personal parcels.

CAPTAIN VICTOR

41 Block to beat 55 block

902 letters came into the Compound yesterd

MOUTHPIECES

Göring, on Hitler's Birth-[day], told the German [pe]ople that "the time [ha]s come for the hard[es]t testing and the de[cis]ive trial of our people [an]d of every German".

D? Goebbels in a speech [on] the 19th, said that the [wa]r had reached its hard-est phase in this 4th year, and nowhere yet can be seen a way out for its end, or the rais-ing of its load and suf-fering.

_____

A U.S.A. Flyer after the daylight on Bremen said "I shall never for-get the air battles, the German aircraft tumbled to the ground like leaves." The Germans say they only lost 2 aircraft.

photographs can be taken at speeds in excess of 200 mph.

The U.S. navy has now started experimenting.

Yesterday evening "Nobby" Hall and several other mem-bers of block 56 were taken before the Officer for playing "darts" and "billiards" on roll-call! The culprits, who asked for an amnesty as it was Hitler's birthday, were pardoned.

COLOUR PHOTOGRAPHY IN WAR

Experiments being car-[rie]d out by the U.S.A. [Ar]my Air Corps, show that [pho]tographs in colour can [al]so be made successfully [i]n aircraft flying more [tha]n 200 miles per hour [an]d at heights ranging

[M]AYBE I WAS "A BIT LOW"-

[up]to about 2 miles.
[I]t has been discovered [tha]t aerial colour photo-[gra]phy can penetrate the [vei]l of camouflage. Var-[ia]tions of shade and tint

are clearly defined: nat-ural colour also gives a sense of depth, or a third dimension. Colour shots can even spot wilted vegetation resulting from a gun blast, although the battery may be dis-guised.

It is about 10 years ago that the National Geographical magazine published the first aerial colour photographs. It was not until 1936, however, that the U.S. Army Air Corps entered into a development and research programme of this branch of photography. The early experiments had to be carried out at 'plane speeds of less than 100 mph. Nowadays successful colour

WANTED

Wanted Oxford Diction-ary or similar, in exchange for Encyclopaedia of uni-versal knowledge.
                    Wiles 55.

The person who borrowed "In the meantime" by Howard Spring, please return to
                Wilkinson 46N.

_____

LOST. A red handled penknife, marked Fripp 46, lost near 56 Block.
                Wimpey.56.

WEATHER FORECAST

Variable skies, but long bright periods between scattered showers. Average temperature.

YESTERDAY'S WEATHER

| MAX. | 52°F | RAIN ·245" |
| MIN. | 46°F | |

PRINTED AND PUBLISHED BY
THE MACKAY BUTCHER PRESS

WORLD WAR NEWS

On Tuesday it was officially announced in London that the whole of the Allied Air Striking Force in the Mediterranean had been re-organised.

Under the command of Air Chief Marshal, Sir A. Teddes, an "Air Force command in the Mediterranean" was formed, consisting of these groups, namely; Middle East Air Chief Marshal Sir Sholto Douglas, in North West Africa, Major General Spaatz, and in Malta, Air Vice Marshal, Sir Keith Park are in command.

Paul Colin, Editor of the German controlled Brussels newspaper "Le Journal Nouveau" was shot whilst leaving his office last week and died as a result of his injuries on the following morning.

Since the German occupation Colin had turned against his own people

and had published scathing attacks on those who did not recognise the new border in Europe.

A decree has been published by General Franco, by which the age groups scheduled for 1944 are to be called up this year.

General Maitland-Wilson, C in C Near East, on a four day visit to Turkey has ratified the deliveries of war material agreed upon at Adana. During his visit, the editor of the official Turkish newspaper, "Ulus" said that Turkey in 1943 had reached an important phase in current events. "It was false to believe that, while great nations were striving for a decision, the peace of Turkey was not in danger. Already the

geographical and strategical position between the Black Sea and the Mediterranean was dangerous. The Turkish people must be stronger than ever behind their leader. He said that the foreign policy of Turkey could not be discussed. "Only let the world know" he ended "that if anyone attacks we shall make the greatest sacrifices".

According to an agreement made by the British Turkish military mission, Turkish flying officers have gone to Cairo for flying instruction

---

Tilsit, Stettin, and Rostock were "blitzed" on the night of April 20th, — 31 aircraft shot down.

After heavy artillery fire strong British forces attacked on the South Tunisian front during the night of the 20th of April.

"BIG EETZ" TO

EANS COMPLETES YEAR AS LEADER

The Barth contingent came into this compound year ago today.

Congratulations to Sgt Deans who has been up Leader since our ival and who has had ry hard and delicate to carry out.

UNITED FRONT

t the present moment s in disgrace and at with the German horities. It is the Compound to back Sgt Deans up to show the Germans t the Camp Leader has full co-operation.

THE "GEN"

"Dixie" was born on an. 1914, is married and no family. In 1936 he ed the R.A.F as a Direct y. was shot down on Sept 1940. Baled out the kite just missed

a Customs house on the Dutch frontier. He spent two holidays in Germany in 1937 and '38.

In his own words he is "flat out for the mob — I know an easy job when I see one!"

CHURCH

Hauptmann Siemoleit has sanctioned the opening of the Theatre on Good Friday and Easter Sunday. Services for Good Friday are as follows:- Morning Prayer 10-30 hours; Evening Prayer 1800 hours, a short service followed by a rendering of the Crucifixion Cantata by the choir. Both services conducted by Capt McConachie, the recently arrived Padre from Schu- bin. On Sunday evening a short service for Anzac day will be held

SHOWER ORGANISER WANTED

The Germans, as long as parties are forthcoming, will provide showers during the summer months. The present N.C.O i/c of showers is resigning. All applicants for this post please hand in their names to the Camp Office.

SPORT

At yesterdays meeting in the Sports store, another appeal was made for the return of missing boots. No boots will be issued until the 20 pairs missing are returned.

Compound Athletics are provisionally fixed for mid-June. Any ideas re events to be handed to sports representatives

CAPTAIN VICTOR

Block 46 to beat Block 42.

Amongst the greatcoats brought into the compound yes- terday for the new arrivals, was a WAAF type coat. This was re- turned to the store!

As tomorrow is Good Friday there will be no issue of "The Daily Recco".

WEATHER

A wedge of high pressure ex- tends from the north. Continuing fine and warm by day. Cool at night.

YESTERDAYS WEATHER
Max 65°F. Min 30°F. Rain:- trace
557 letters in yesterday.

RESCUE

PRINTED AND PUBLISHED BY THE MACKAY BUTCHER PRESS

JAPAN TAKES REPRISALS

AMERICANS EXECUTED

On the 18th April, 1942, American airmen attacked Tokio, and, as the Japanese Government asserted, committed "inhuman acts" against the civilian population. A number of the airmen, taken prisoner, were brought before a court martial and sentenced to death. On the 9th of March 1943, the Japanese Government sent a note to the American Government, in which the following paragraphs were contained.

RESPECTING HUMANITY

It is the intention of the Imperial Japanese Gov't to bring those members of the crews of enemy aircraft before a court martial, and punish them severely as enemies of humanity, who, after an air attack on Japanese territory, manchukuo or areas under Japanese military occupation, fall under Japanese authority and after examination are found guilty of acts of cruelty and inhumanity. The Japanese Government however, has no intention of inflicting heavy punishment merely for "participation in military operations" as the American Government asserts. The measures of the Japanese Government are based on the moral idea of the necessity of respecting humanity and limiting the victims of the war to a minimum

CHILDREN KILLED

Members of the crews of American aircraft who, after an air attack on Japan, fell under Japanese authority, purposely bombed, or set fire to, such non-military objects as hospitals and schools, and have shot at civilians, who were a long way from military targets. It is especially noteworthy that they machine-gunned innocent children who were playing in the school yard and killed or wounded them after they had clearly recognised them as children. The above members of the crew admitted these facts and asserted that such an act was only natural and insisted on the correctness of their attitude. The American Government must understand fully and completely that such men are enemies of humanity and are criminals who cannot be pardoned. The Japanese Government will not treat such criminals as prisoners of war.

DEATH SENTENCE

As the guilt of these men had been clearly proved, they were, in conformity with military laws, sentenced to death. For the majority, however, the sentence was specially changed. The death sentence was only employed for a few of them. The Japanese Government intends only such members of aircraft crews who, after air attack on Japan, manchukuo or Japanese occupied territory

...l into Japanese hands ...d have committed no ...el and inhuman acts, ...e prisoners of war.

PROTEST

On the 24th April, 1943, a ...test dated 12th April 1943 ...s received in Tokio, from ...American Government ...which they accuse Japan ...infringing the Geneva ...vention for prisoners of ...r. Japan replied that ...this affair their attitude ...s quite clear. In the ...ditional spirit of the ...ushido", and in conformity ...th their ideals, which made ...m always ready to ...tow upon their enemies ...agnanimous and humane ...atment, it could not be ...nded to soldiers who com- ...itted inhumane acts of ...uelty simply because ...y were wearing military ...forms. The Japanese ...ers printed detailed ...tracts from the American ...ports of the first attack on ...kio, and say these reports ...present only a confirmat- ...n of the previous Japan- ...se declarations, and is ...y new proof delivered by ...a Americans themselves.

PITOPOLY

Following the news, that new arrivals were expected in the camp, from Dulag, a new craze hit the Compound at the week-end.

Large scrolls of paper were in evidence with plans of blocks carefully drawn out. Small slips of pasteboard, representing beds, were then meticulous- ly laid on the plan. The game was open to any number, the idea being to arrange the beds so that everyone was happy!

In Block 42, a huge crowd could be seen at any hour of the day milling round the board. During the opening skirmishes such cries as "not there, you fool!" "no, that's mine!" and "Its your move now" could be heard from the fringe of the crowd.

Several hours later new combatants entered the lists and the fun started all over again.

Late last night after much turmoil a state of com- parative calm existed. One member of the block, when the "bedlam" had subsided, was heard to murmur cynic- -ally.

"never was so much moved around by so many for so little!"

COMPETITION

The competition publish- ed in yesterday's paper was won by Moffat (41). The correct result was brought in at 10.30 hrs yesterday morning.

To save any further brain fag Smith is the engineer.

CAPTAIN VICTOR

Block 44 to beat Block 40.

WANTED

Two pairs of summer underpants in exchange for cigarettes.
Recco Box no 36

WEATHER FORECAST

none forthcoming.

120.
PRINTED AND PUBLISHED BY
THE MACKAY BUTCHER PRESS.

NEWS RESTRICTIO

TOC H CIGARETTE SCHEME

In keeping with the "world wide" help thy neighbour" policy of the Toc H, the members of the Stalag Luft 3 branch have issued an appeal to the whole compound for cigarettes and tobacco in order to help new prisoners and the few more unfortunate older "Kriegies" to eke out their Red Cross issue.

There was a magnificent response to their experimental appeal in 39 Block, 3,865 cigarettes and 8 ozs. of tobacco being collected. Encouraged by this success, the Toc H representatives of the various blocks will make a similar collection during the next few days.

The collection and distribution of these cigarettes will be the sole responsibility of the Toc H,

who will periodically issue balance sheets. Each needy case will be thouroughly, but discreetly, enquired into. The issues will not be prodigal, but the scheme will ensure that every prisoner has an adequate supply of smokes.

The justice of this scheme will surely be apparent to all those men who have more than they need, and we feel confident that there will be a ready response.

Remember: One day your parcels may go astray!

CAPTAIN VICTOR

56 Block to beat 55 block

211 letters came into the compound yesterday.

It is with editors of the "Da ing to tell their re our last issue will the Germans will c sent to raise certai banps on our source of news.

At the conferen with the Kommand yesterday Sgt. Dean was informed that Camp newspaper wo be tolerated only on following conditions.

1. No political stories must be publishe
2. The sheet would c tain no war news
3. Camp politics (i.e. lations with the G mans) are forbidde
4. Before publication the paper is to be c sored by a Germa officer.

Under these conditio

S SPELL FINISH

regret that the
cco" have this morn-
that this will be

know from exper-
ce that it would
impossible to produce
daily newspaper of
y sustained interest;
three news sources
uned represent at
quent periods 75%
our copy.

We can only hope
at if the authorities
ll condescend to per-
e our previous 63
nes – which have
parently given no
use for complaint
they will see their
y clear to allow us
continue as before.

ENTERTAINMENT

At a meeting of the E.C. yesterday evening, it was decided to continue with the programme as planned, beginning with "Home and Beauty" on Monday next. Notices re the completion of booking for this show will be issued in due course.

The future programme is provisionally as follows:

May. 24th Dance band.
June 7th Thro' the music sheet.
June 21st Mikado
July 5th Thunder Rock
July 12th Theatre Orchestra
July 26th Variety
Aug. 2nd Orchestral Concert
Aug. 16th The man who came to dinner.

This coming Sunday evening at 19.15 hours will be a recital of swing re-cords.

It is hoped that hired costumes will once more be available for future shows.

Anyone amongst the new arrivals or anyone at all, who can play a musical instrument, whether dance or orchest-ral, is invited to see Sgt. Fender. Block 45.

"DIXIE" DEANS

We feel sure the Compound is behind us when we publicly thank Sgt. Deans for the part he has played in the recent negotiations with the authorities. In addition on behalf of the whole camp we congratulate the Camp Leader on the able man-ner in which he has carried out his year of duties.

WEATHER FORECAST

An anticyclone is centred in the North. Continuing mainly fair, with gusty Easterly wind and average temperature by day. Cool at night.

YESTERDAY'S WEATHER
MAX. 54°F MIN. 37°F. Rain. NIL

PRINTED AND PUBLISHED BY
THE MACKAY BUTCHER PRESS.

Central Europe with 1939 Borders

showing the location of the main camps in this story

Prisoners were periodically transported from camp to camp. Alan Mackay
spent the last weeks of the war marching round the Lüneberg Heath after
leaving the camp at Fallingbostel. It was from this march that he made
his escape

Dulag Luft (Durchgangslager der Luftwaffe) a reception camp near
Frankfurt am Main

Barth was on the shores of the Baltic near to the Peenemunde rocket
test range

Sagan was the location of the Great Escape of officers

Thorn was a short stay transit camp

Heydekrug was near the Lithuanian border

Fallingbostel was just a few miles from Belsen where Alan Mackay saw
concentration camp prisoners in striped uniforms

Front Gunner
Forward, coldly, twin guns
Searching, eager;
Above, scraped clouds, a star,
Dreams.
Behind, five lives, living;
Each second vital, full,
Dry-mouthed expectancy.
Below, a river thickly twisting,
Grain fields, mellow,
Homes.
Watching, waiting, thinking
Of tomorrow's leave,
Home, wife, son,
Fireside dispelling shrouds
Of war.
But now, a job.

Pilot
Pilot, mind clear, icy;
Engines, heart, pulsing;
Man and machine commingling;
Check gauges, compass;
Flak spuming, futile,
Laugh youth.
Bombs gone, a hit,
Enraged guns vomit death,
Dodge and laugh.
Jar of shells
Against living metal;
Fabric ripped – trailing,
Forlorn pennant
Of glorious endeavour.

Observer
Spread-eagled, downwards peering,
Checking, judging, timing.
Left, left, steady.
One touch releasing
Death's tools, ungainly,
Spewed forth, horribly,
Carrying hatred, maiming,
Warped buildings
Over warped bodies,
Mangled fingers, accusing,
Pointing upwards.
Target bombed, course home,
Mind, pencil, busy–
Office job in jaws
Of chaos.

New Walls

The death of the *Recco* at Sagan was, as we promised ourselves, followed by a holiday for the editorial staff and, shortly afterwards, a transfer of the whole camp to Heydekrug.

It was there, finding time hanging heavily on my hands, that I penned a collection of verses describing in poetic form, the feelings of a typical bomber crew on operations. I sent them home to my former boss Frank Gray. He thought they were good enough to be published in the *People's Journal* of March 18 1944.

But once the poetry-writing bug and the novelty of our new surroundings had worn off – it must have lasted for a whole week – I once again felt the itch to get the *Recco* back on the barrack wall. The itch was helped along by frequent requests from my fellow prisoners to get the presses rolling again. They were missing their daily ration of news and gossip which helped take their minds off their daily rations.

Bill Butcher, enjoying his new-found freedom, was no longer interested in the joint editorship and graciously declined the invitation to join the editorial board – a new trestle table in an even more crowded barrack. However, Australian Dennis Adams, expressing more than a passing interest in the project, was recruited and helped produce the *Recco*'s second run which started on January 31, 1944. Yes!, we had missed another 'Home for Christmas'. Sgt. Adams however lasted only until March 9, when he left to start up his own Sunday paper. Into the breach stepped Stanley 'Joe' Whitlock who lasted until the final closedown of the *Recco* on May 1, 1944, bearing stoically with me the temporary close-downs and censorship imposed by our German captors.

But the new-look *Recco* started with one great advantage over its predecessor – both for the editors and the readers – it was typewritten. The German typewriter, kindly provided by the Kommandant through Dixie Deans' good offices (Could it also have been so that his goons could better censor the finished product?) eased our aching fingers and, I am sure, reduced the eyestrain suffered by our regular readers. The print, in addition, was not so susceptible to being washed out by rain showers so that it was still legible when we took it down at night.

In our first edition, carrying a cartoon from Big Eetz stating that he was leaving winter hibernation and carrying the information that there were only 330 days to Christmas, we announced:

DAILY RECCO REVIVED
BIG EETZ BACK

The first edition also carried the information that the camp was suffering from a major outbreak of 'flu'.

FLU EPIDEMIC
HOME GARGLES

The new paper got off to a flying start and we found we had even more readers than at Sagan. This didn't necessarily mean that we had educated our public into a greater awareness of what was going on, nor that the readership had improved their own capabilities in the search for knowledge.

It simply meant that more and more aircrew were being shot down and processed through the German Prison Camp system. But despite the influx of new blood we had to repeat the old Sagan story of appealing to our public to let us – and through us the rest of the camp – know what was going on.

WHAT DO YOU KNOW?

Production even in peacetime of a daily newspaper is not without its difficulties and in wartime these difficulties are increased to such an extent as to turn even the most hardened newspapermen grey with anxiety. Censorship, shortage of staff, newsprint restrictions, lack of space, air raids, to mention but a few, are some of the many problems that face the wartime editor.
Add to these the difficulties attending running a daily, not only inside Germany, but inside barbed wire and you will understand why the *Recco* feels bound to ask in advance for the indulgence of its readers if at any future date an issue or two should appear a trifle dull.

RECCO'S DIFFICULTIES

This week the *Recco* goes joyously to press, full of the new life of resurrection but those who remember our Sagan history will know that at certain times it is necessary to step warily, even to the extent of vagueness, in the recording of camp events. It is as well to be prepared for a repetition of such times.
From bitter experience the editors also know that the occasions will crop up when the compound will appear to be dead as far as news-gathering is concerned. It is then that they really despair, because they are quite aware of the fact that it is impossible for over 3,000 men to go through the normal

The new-look Recco started in Heydekrug with one great advantage over its predecessor – both for the editors and the readers – it was typewritten

Daily Recco

330 DAYS TO CHRISTMAS.   Roll-Call - 9.00 & 2.00.   ISSUE No. 1.

Monday, 31st. January, 1944.

WEATHER
Yesterday's Temperatures
Max.   41deg. F.
Min.   40deg. F.

Y RECCO REVIVED

BIG EETZ BACK

It appears that the Urge of Spring, the desire to be up and doing and so on, awakens in our blood quicker than it does in the blood of normal people.

Last year on the 15th. of February, this uprising of the Spirit took the form of "The Daily RecoO". We beat our own record this year by going to print on the 30th. of January. Like Big Eetz we are coming out of our winter quarters full of bright ideas.

At Sagan our principles were simple and straight forward. These aims are before us now. For those of you who are for the first time readers of "The Daily RecoO", we shall again outline our tenets: To give the latest Home and Foreign News; To keep you informed of all that is happening in the way of Entertainments, Sport, Education, etc.; To squash all malignant rumours; and To give interesting and amusing extracts from mail.

In short to put before you in condensed form an informative and amusing newspaper.

To Editor 'Daily Recco'
Just leaving winter quarters
— arrive Wednesday. — B Eetz.

If you have any ideas, problems, or queries, bring them to Sgt. A. Mackay, B9, or to Sgt. D. Adams, A3. We depend upon you for News.

SPORTSMEN TO PLAY EITHER SOCCER OR RUGBY - NOT BOTH?

MORE GAMES FOR EVERYONE

At a recent meeting of the Football Cttee. F/Sgt. J.Bryce was elected Pres. The following are the officials: Pres.-J.Bryce, Vice-Pres.-D.Storer,Sec.-A.Fuce,cttee: Messrs.Lynn, A.Smith & Brotherton.

On taking over the presidency yesterday afternoon F/Sgt. Bryce reviewed last season's activities.

In his résumé the president announced that 82 teams participated in all the leagues. The major teams, approx. 10%, played 1 game per week on the wishes of the compound. The remaining 90% played at a maximum 1 game per fortnight.

F/Sgt, Bryce thought this rather rough on the 90% and to alleviate this suggested that all people participating in sport, play either Rugger or Soccer.

The Pres. expressed the hope that the matter would be solved without having to report to his suggestion. The matter is being taken up by the respective cttees.

Periods at present will be short but it is pointed out that the nights are drawing out and in the near future more games will be played each day.

Spectators are requested not to stand against the Entertainments Hut while shows are in progress.

All Soccer Reps. are requested to collect football boots from the Sports Store between 10 and 12 this morning.

CATERING

If you do not need the Argentine Margarine which will be issued this week you are asked to hand it to the Cook-house.

There will be no Coffee brew on Tuesday and Thursday mid-day this week.

Used fat for use in lamps can be obtained from the Cook-house.

MENU
A & C - Egg.
B & D - Brit. Mt. Roll Hash & Eng. Veg.

A & C - Bully Hash.
B & D - Egg.

MUSIC

The Musical Appreciation Class will be held as usual to-day at 15.30 hrs. in the Fiction Library. Stools are required. Please be punctual.

COMPETITION
Watch to-morrow's Edition for full Competition details.

Printed and Published by the MacAdam Press.

routine of living without something happening which could be news as far as their columns are concerned. In other words they must print a lifeless newssheet merely because the live incidents of the day have been allowed to pass unrecorded.

Obviously the *Recco* cannot employ a huge staff of reporters to pry into every concern in the camp – that would be undesirable anyway. It is possible, however, for the compound as a whole to become news-minded and for any individual to acquaint the editor of any incident of which he happens to have heard. Nature notes, plant life, if any in this drab place; accidents, humorous or otherwise; inaugurations of new societies, business of established ones; lines of new Kriegies; mail gen – in fact anything that might appear to be possible material for their columns.

The *Daily Recco* want to present a lively daily newssheet and with your cooperation we know this is possible.

But thirteen issues later on February 19, we were forced, through lack of hard copy, to fill in space by giving a facetious account of a typical day in the life of the *Recco*'s editorial staff.

MEMORANDUM OF MUGS

Underneath we give you an example of a typical day in the life of the editorial staff of the *Daily Recco*.

08.40 Get up. 08.45 Breakfast. 08.50 Get down.

08.58 Get up. 09.00 Parade. 09.30 Paper is published. 09.45 Think up article for next day's issue. 10.00 Still thinking. 10.15 Establish communications with E and K lagers. 10.30 Brew. 10.45 Back to article. Plan layout. 11.00 Scrap layout and get new one. 11.15 Foreign correspondent brings in new article – change layout. 11.30 Scouts scout and cub reporter reports. 11.45 Collect wits. 12.00 Start typing.

12.30 Finish typing – Lunch. 12.45 Think of headings and get Whitlock Press organised.

13.00 Press thinks of headings; editor disorganised. 13.15 Interview with disillusioned reporter – fired. 13.10 Overseas paper published.

13.45 Get ready for parade. 14.00 parade. 14.25

Get over parade. 14.30 Brew. 14.45 Contact various departments for gen.

15.20 Still contacting. 15.30 Nothing to fill paper – panic.

16.00 Tea. 16.30 Constant stream of wanted and lost customers. 17.30 Rest.

18.30 Still resting.

18.45 Start typing. 19.00 Completely alter layout to cope with fresh news.

20.00 Finish typing.

20.30 Supper 21.00 Conference with Whitlock Press. 21.30 Press starts working. 22.30 Press still working. 23.00 Lights out – bed. 23.30 What will tomorrow's article be? 23.59 Dreaming.

03.00 Get up. 03.02 Get down. 08.40 Still Dreaming. 08.41 Another day.

A few issues prior to that heart-rending account of our daily lives we published an article on the forces newspaper the Union Jack, edited at that

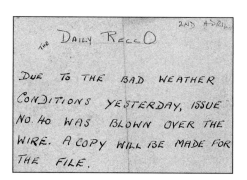

SUNDAY. 28ᵗʰ FEBRUARY. 1943.

SPECIAL EDITION

OF

THE DAILY RECCO

ATTEMPTED ESCAPE

About 20.30 hours last night Sgts. Saxton and Joyce of 55 Block attempted to make a break. According to a report they were picked up by search lights near the South wire. An unteroffizer called on them to "stand-up." Sgt. Saxton did so but Sgt. Joyce laid still. Guns opened up and Sgt. Joyce was hit twice in the fore-arm and once in the upper arm. A bullet also scraped an ear.

He was taken to sick-bay where he had a bad night due to pain. His condition should not prove serious.

PRINTED AND PUBLISHED BY 128.
THE MACKAY BUTCHER PRESS

Daily troubles
April 2, 1943 (left);
February 28, 1943 (right)

time by Hugh Cudlipp whose later philosophy of 'publish and be damned' we had pre-empted in our battle with the German camp authorities. The brashness of our opening sentence in the article would have appealed, I am sure, to the Fleet Street tycoon – if he had known about it.

UNION JACK GIVES
FIGHTING TROOPS ALL
LATEST BATTLE NEWS

After the *Daily Recco*, one of the most unusual newspapers in the world is the *Union Jack*, published at Constantine halfway between Tunis and Algiers; it is an official British Army publication … A newspaper which is sold to troops serving in Africa and fighting on the Mediterranean front.

During the Sicilian campaign, native youths in Syracuse, Augusta, Marsala and other towns were selling editions of *Union Jack* even as British troops were occupying these towns.

Already this British Army newspaper unit is running an additional evening paper which is sold in each town occupied by British troops.

All *Union Jack* writers and printers are professional newspapermen and they retain their trade in the army. War correspondents lend a willing hand giving the troops the finest front-line news service of any paper in the world. Teleprinter, cable, radio and telephone are used and its distribution by aeroplane must surely be unique in newspaper history.

Chief editor of *Union Jack* and all Allied publications is Capt. Hugh Cudlipp, peacetime editor of the *Sunday Pictorial* who, after serving with the armoured division during the Tunisian campaign, was placed in charge of *Union Jack*.

This unusual paper is not a Wall paper like the *Daily Recco*, neither is it in any shape or form an underground one. It is a properly printed newspaper which is sold for general circulation.

Union Jack, *Daily Recco* and *Hobo news* are probably the three strangest newspapers in the world today.

Debate

From the outside all the barracks looked the same, with the same wooden shutters which were banged shut and bolted from the outside at night by the German guards patrolling the compound with their dogs. But inside they were completely different. Some were permanently clean with scrubbed floors and table-tops showing that the block leader, supported by the inmates, believed in everything being shipshape and Bristol fashion. Others, not necessarily more appealing, had a much more lived-in look, an air of comfortable untidiness, partly caused by the bodies seemingly permanently sprawled in the two-tier pits. In others the standard symmetry and conformity of the beds had been cunningly altered to form little enclaves in which an entire combine could be isolated from the rest of their comrades – if that was what they wanted.

In some, Red Cross packing cases had been fashioned into more or less comfortable armchairs, with ordinary cardboard parcel containers fashioned into cupboards, display cabinets and lockers for the little world of photographs, letters and souvenirs which acted as a permanent reminder to the owner that there actually was another world away from the camp.

At any hour of the day or night until lights out, Kriegies could be seen sitting at the tables or on their beds, studying, reading, making models, pursuing hobbies, playing chess, draughts, and cards or simply talking and arguing. Discussion ranged far and wide, covering memories of home, plans for the future (always rosy), local habits and customs, ancestry, religion, politics, women (they cropped up no matter the subject), morality and the every day community life of the barrack and the camp. And, every day, a principal topic was the progress of the war and the hoped-for date of the end.

Occasionally the barrack-room debates were aired on the wider stage of the camp debating society. One discussion which created a lot of interest – during the debate and after – was the international armaments race. A discussion in our own block on the issue and on the morality – or absence of morality – among arms dealers persuaded us that we should open up the discussion to the whole camp through the *Recco*.

On March 28, 1944 we published:

THE ARMS RACE
FACTS AND FIGURES ON THE ARMS RACE

At the inter-compound debate last week the points raised on the armament race caused a certain amount of interest. We have decided to publish a fuller account of the powers behind the war.

In the period preceding the war there was nothing in Europe that could be called an armaments ring. But without a shadow of doubt, there was a huge and subversive force that lay behind the arming and counter-arming of the nations.

Vickers-Armstrong

Chairman, Gen. the Hon. Sir Herbert Lawrence CGB, one-time Chief of Staff of the B.F., has put himself on record as stating Vickers-Armstrong Ltd relies very heavily on armament orders for its existence.

It has factories in Rumania, where, for greater convenience, Sir H. Lawrence is a Director of the Bank of Rumania.

There are also Vickers factories or subsidiaries in Italy, Japan, Spain, Canada, Ireland, Holland and New Zealand. Sir Otto Niemeyer of the Bank of England is another Vickers director.

Among the more prominent share holders in 1932 of Vickers or associated concerns were the Rt. Hon. Neville Chamberlain and Sir Austin Chamberlain M.P. winner of the Nobel Peace Prize, 1925. In 1914 the list was even more imposing. It included Lord Balfour, Lord Curzon and also Lord Kinnaird (Pres. of the YMCA). Three Bishops and Dean Inge of St. Paul's were also included.

Sir Basil Zaharoff

Mr Basileios Zacharias, the greatest arms salesman this world has ever known, enjoyed the distinction of having sold the first practical submarine ever used in naval operations to his native Greece and the further distinction of having used this sale to frighten Turkey into buying two submarines. The Boer War added to his laurels;.

Boers shot Englishmen with Vickers guns and ammunition. The Russo-Japanese war provided him with an ever wider field for his gifts. Vickers sold as much and possibly more war material to Russia than it did to England's supposed ally Japan.

In 1917 when there seemed a possibility of peace through the intervention of the USA, Lord Bertie, Ambassador to France, naively recorded in his diary Zaharoff is all for continuing the war to the end.

Charles P.E. Schneider

A man of many offices – the executive head of armament firms throughout Europe – President of the Schneider-Creusot company, armament manufacturers. He is a director or the *Banque de L'union Parisienne*, one of whose most profitable sources of business was the financing of loans for armaments. In 1920 he founded and became President of the *Union Europeanne Industriale et Financiers*. Through it Schneider-Creusot controls 182 French companies manufacturing heavy ordnance, machine guns, tanks, shells, ammunition and warfare chemicals. But the *Union Europeanne* has an even more important function. Through it Schneider-Creusot reaches out to control 230 armament and allied enterprises outside France.

The greatest of these concerns is Skoda which has factories scattered, not only in Czechoslovakia, but over Poland and Rumania as well. Upon the Skoda board controlled by UE through 56% of its stock, Mrs. Schneider sits with, among others, Eduard Benes who takes second place to no-one in the vocal support he lent to the League of Nations. Also two Czech-Germans von Dutschnitz and von Arthaber who were very heavy financial contributors to Hitler's political success.

This article will be continued in tomorrow's edition.

MORE ARMS DISCLOSURES

CONTINUING WITH OUR ARTICLES OF
YESTERDAY'S EDITION WE WILL DEAL TODAY
WITH TWO MORE OF THE INTERNATIONAL
FIRMS IN THE ARMAMENTS RAMP

Comite des Forges de France far overtopping Schnieider-Creusot – the most powerful iron and steel organisation in France – 250 companies made up its membership of which 150 were armament concerns. It does not sell, it does not produce. It controls the press: it has the ear of the Foreign Office. Its President is Francois de Wendel, the members of whose family have always been uniquely international. When their vast Lorraine estates lay upon soil politically German, they attached to their name the prefix von and turned their eyes towards Berlin. When the political frontier again shifted over their rich deposits of coal and iron they altered the prefix to de and looked to Paris.

In 1914 the ranking member of the family was Humbert von Wendel a member of the German Reichstag. A younger brother Guy was a French senator.

When a military advance turned a French possession into a German one the de Wendels felt no great concern. Regardless of the national tag attached to these mines and steelworks, they remained in placid control of one or other branches of the family.

Francois de Wendel President of the C. de F., Regent of the Banque de France, member of the Chamber of Deputies for Meurthe and Moselle owned a majority interest in Le Journal des Debats which was the head of the group that in October 1931 purchased the semi-official newspaper of the French Government Le Temps.

It controlled the Journee Industrielle and was a power in the management of Le Matin and L'Echo de Paris.

Yet for all the illustriousness of this multi-sided man, the newspapers of France almost never mentioned his name. He did not like publicity.

Fritz Thyssen

The head of Vereinigte Stahlwerg A-G. In 1932 he made a single contribution of three million marks for the presidential campaign.

The leading armament makers, not only in Germany but in France, united in their support behind the new leader. By a curious coincidence the de Wendel-controlled newspapers in Paris immediately broke out in a fever of denunciation against the new regime and called for fresh guarantees of security against the re-armament of Germany.

Armament Salesmanship

The armament industry operates with one curious advantage over any other business in the world;

the greater the competition the greater amount of business for all competitors. Salesmen for the armament industry know the fact well and build on it. If a SOC salesman sold 100,000 rifles to Yugoslavia, he had already eased the path of the V-A salesman in selling 200,000 rifles to Italy.

The Great War

Throughout the Great War English and French industries maintained to Germany a steady stream of glycerine, nickel, copper, oil and rubber. Germany returned the compliment; she sent to France iron, steel and magnetos for petrol engines.

Rear-admiral M.W.P. Cousett who was British Naval Attaché in Denmark and later in Norway and Sweden stated in so many words that if the blockade of Germany had been really effective during 1915-16 Germany would have been forced to her knees. And it is he who is also responsible for the statement In 1915, England exported twice as much nickel to Sweden than in the previous two years put together.

Regarding the immunity from bombing of Briey, this statement was made by Deputy Barthe in the Chamber on January 24th 1919.

"I affirm that either by the factor of the international solidarity of the great metallurgy companies or in order to safeguard private business interests, our military chiefs were ordered not to bombard the establishments in the Briey basin which were being exploited by the enemy.

"I affirm that our aviation service received instructions to respect the blast furnaces in which enemy steel was being made and that a General who wished to bombard them was reprimanded."

The articles, as was intended, got everyone talking. In Kriegie camp we had time to think, dispassionately in the main, and with some personal and often hurtful knowledge, about arms manufacture and the morality of starting up a company with the sole purpose of making instruments which will kill, whose sole purpose is to kill, and which are designed to kill more efficiently than any weapons already in existence.

Ironically, nearly forty years after we published our articles in the *Recco*, the British public, mourning their dead in the Falklands war, were told the British soldiers, sailors and airmen had been attacked, maimed and killed by weapons supplied by, among others, the British, American and French governments to the Argentinians. What we tried to point out all those years ago in the *Recco*, and it has been borne out since then by the cynical attitude of the Americans and Russians principally although not solely, is that bigger and better weapons, either conventional or nuclear, do not deter.

They merely lead to bigger and better tools of destruction. And some day, somewhere, some bully boy will want, or will feel fireproof enough, to test them out in action.

Shortly before we widened the debate on the arms race we triggered off another major camp discussion on February 29, when we printed a leading article on the morality of war itself.

MAN'S INHUMANITY TO MAN

Why should we suffer?, the old, old cry of the peoples of any nation involved in war. The keynote of all the struggles of the years from the dark ages to the present time when it is raised from the stricken towns of Europe under the blows of air warfare.

However, the onus of war rests with the masses who suffer themselves to be led by men in whom they blindly lay their confidence. As long as their path is peaceful they are contented, but if they are plunged into a war why should they, in their own stupidity, follow their leaders blindly?

Surely no political system can be so rigidly maintained that it will stand firm against a tide of opposition trying to sweep it away.

One of the main arguments against bombing is that it is not chivalrous – is there such a quality as chivalry? Possibly in isolated cases but in the main we tend to be influenced by historical fiction which conveniently omits and alters the true facts of war.

Then again, women and children must be spared – they can be spared if they are evacuated. Those men and women whose interests keep them in the towns are helping the war effort: munitions workers, clerks etc, who are concerned with war production are military targets.

Immediately after consolidating her new positions in the occupied countries, Germany flung her bombing planes at London and other industrial towns, the nerve centres of the Allied war effort, in an effort to shorten the war. With this philosophy she justified herself and indeed boasted of it to the extent of coining a new verb – to coventrate.

Now that the Allies are using the air weapon to its full extent, the German press by a similar method to that of the Allies, describes them as terror raiders and air gangsters in order to transmute the self-pity of the masses into hate.

But inhuman though air bombing is to the recipients, if it shortens the war, let both continue to use it and take their own precautions for the protection of innocents until their peoples awake from their propaganda-drugged trance to cry Halt!

The reaction was a series of hotly-argued debates in barrack rooms all over the camp with, even, some of our readers paying a personal call to say just what they thought about the article – both pro and con. We might have followed up immediately with another similar thought-piece, but the next day's issue carried the startling news that the camp was to hold 8,000 prisoners. We had a new and much more personal topic of conversation.

But we did get back to the subject on March 23.

POWER CAUSETH PEACE FINALLY

Readers of last Tuesday's issue of the *Daily Recco* will realise that the story of the Krupps marvel lost nothing by the handling it received from the Allied press, but it must be remembered that, in the country of its origin, it was accepted with all the simplicity and hopefulness, that similar stories are today.

Poor Substitute

The past year of withdrawals according to plan
has not only tested the Elastic defences of the German forces, but the ingenuity of the German Ministry of Propaganda. The man who can turn the loss of hundreds of miles of terrain into a succession of Glorious Victories must elicit a certain amount of admiration – even from his country's enemies. However, we feel that, at its best, propaganda is a poor substitute for force.

Cold Comfort

The people in the best position to judge the value of propaganda are the inhabitants of the German towns who, at the beginning of the war, ridiculed the British leaflets bearing the words This might have been a bomb: today as they sit in their shelters listening to the heavy-calibre bombs falling on their homes, it must be cold comfort indeed for them to think These may have been leaflets.

Its Value

Propaganda can, and does, play an important part in marshalling pubic opinion behind the Government; it can be used to gloss over setbacks, to stiffen morale and in many other ways.

Although the victor of many paper battles it can never win a war on its own.

Right alongside the leader we carried a full column of war news which graphically illustrated the very point we had been making.

SCHMERINKA EVACUATED

THE GERMAN RADIO REPORTED YESTERDAY THAT:

On the lower Bug strong Russian forces attacked several German positions unsuccessfully.

Between the middle Bug and the Dniester heavy battles continue with superior Soviet forces. The city of Schmerinka was evacuated according to plan.

The Soviets have recommenced their offensive with strong infantry and tank forces between Tarnapol and Proscurow. In the heavy fighting 3 Soviet tanks were destroyed. In the Brody area German troops are engaged in heavy offensive fighting with the advancing Soviets. German defence forces in Kowel repulsed repeated Soviet attacks.

S.E of Witebsk, the Soviets renewed violent breakthrough efforts with strong infantry and tank forces. German forces repulsed all attacks and blocked a local breech.

In Italy there were renewed allied attacks on Cassino. German long-range guns damaged a freighter off the beach-heads on the Nettuno and Anzio.

German coastal batteries on the Adriatic shelled 2 enemy destroyers, setting one on fire and forcing the other to draw off.

German bombers made another great attack on London last night. Large quantities of H.E. and incendiary bombs were dropped causing extensive fires and damage.

German long-range batteries on the French coast shelled Dover with observed good effect.

Carrying reflective 'think pieces' about the ethics of arms trading was interrupted on March 1, 1944 with the news of a major expansion in prisoner numbers (below)

(overleaf) American School of Murder – a report of the Volkischer Beobachter's view of the British and the Americans

Daily Reeed

Issue No. 27

"Freedom and Boat"
300 Days to Christmass

Roll Call 0900 and 1400

Wednesday 1ˢᵗ March 1944

1 8,000

Commandant

es attended the Conference with ernoon when the following points

RE- HAD ECT- NG A AND BE RT OF OT AG- R CLI- ER HE WHICH N AUTH E TO. EMOVED THEY

eetin 's r was

THE COMMANDANT AGREED TO ALLOW VISITORS FROM 2 AND3 LAGERS TO LAGER 1, NEXT WEEK-END FOR RUGBY AND FOOT BALL GAMES. HE WOULD ALLOW 100 VISITORS FROM THE TWO LAGERS IN ADDITION TO THE TEAMS+ HE ASKED SGT. DEANS TO GIVE HIS WORD THAT THERE WOULD BE NO EXCHANGES.

Oberst Von Hörmann said that he would see if the German Menu could be provided each week and he point edcout that the Menu depend

ed tha into e said no- stated re to s oc-

ed upon the produce which was obtainable locally.

Sgt. Deans stated that recently when potatoes arrived in Lager 1, they arrived so early in the morning that no men were available for unloading them. The potatoes were taken out again. It would have been possible for a workparty to have been there if warning had been given. He noticed that a similar incident had occurred in Lager 3. In reply, the Commandant promised to investigate the matter.

ted uf- omp- den the ege- n the said the

rette er the rink- eison- rlager be

The Commandant announced that by Wednesday the Arres tlock would be nearly empty. He hoped that this happy state of affairs would continue.

The Oberst expressed his pleasure at the clean and tidy state of Lager 2, and congratulated the Compound Leader, Sgt. Paules.

Cook-house

The following is a list of the meats received in the N.Z. parcels this week:
Corned Meats, 1 lb.   575.
Roast Beef   "   93.
Boiled Beef   "   260.
Corned Meats 12ozs.   517.
Lamb & Peas   "   356.
Tongue   "   106.
Tomatoes & Sausages.
                15oz.   8.
Lamb & Tomatoes 16oz. 15.
Rabbit & Bac on "   9.
Frankfurter & Veg. 12oz.3.

Owing to the odd quantities, people must make the chance of receiving odd meals. The ration for 1 lb tins is one fifth per man and for 12oz. tins - a quarter per man

M E N U
ALL CAMP - Sardines.

ALL CAMP - German Stew.

Mail

The box of mail which arrived yesterday contained 2722 letters. They have all been distributed.
There are now 2 boxes in transit.

Paper Shortage

A letter has been received from the Y.M.C.A Depot at Sagan stating that they have received a large order which was sent to them in the middle of December and which they forwarded to Sweden.

As this order cannot be fulfilled until at the earliest the middle of April, and as the existing stocks are only sufficient on the present basis, to last a fortnight or three weeks, you are asked to co-operate by conserving supplies and any scraps you can get hold of in lieu of good paper.

Motor Sports Club

Members of the above Club are reminded to have their nominations for new officers in before Friday. Officials are: President, Secretary, and 4 committee members.

Toc. H.

Members and probationers please note that the meeting for this week is cancelled.

Lost

One rubber heel on the circuit.
POLMEER   B 9.

A pair of suede flying boots were taken from the wash-house by mistake at 10.30 am., Monday. Please return to
INGGS   A 2.

Wanted

Wanted pipe and tobacco or pipe and chocolate for size 9 suede flying boots.
BROWN   D 4.

Wanted one-act German plays.
RICE   B 7.

Wanted Spanish-English or English-Spanish Dictionary. for any reasonable offer.
JACKMAN   D 8.

Wanted French Dictionary for "Practical Maths. for all"
CHURCH   C 11.

Don't have long drawn-out arguments in your rooms. Bring your queries to the Daily Reeed Information Bureau.

What to do with Back-Pay

This advice is offered for the post-war period when European Countries will try to raise loans in England for the re-construction of their State. It is a matter of pride that Great Britain, was a country who was hard-hit by the last war and who paid her obligations in full. The moral is obvious.

Far better for British investors to accept a smaller interest by dealing with somebody who will give them a square deal rather than with somebody else who offers a big yield and a bigger risk.

It is the small investor who is caught every time. It is your money which is lost, not the big money. You are the first in and the last out. When settlements are made on a new basis the small investor is not consulted at all. The big financiers may decide to accept a quarter of what you originally paid in settlement, of say, Turkey's outstanding debt, at the same time floating a new loan for it.

My advice, therefore, is to have nothing to do with foreign currency bonds. BUY BRITISH.

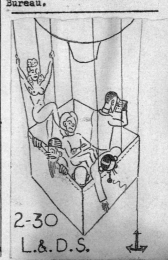

2-30

L.&.D.S.

from our Mail Bag

"... I have just bought 2 Towels, 6 Handkerchiefs and 2 Black Ties for your parcel. They cost 28 shillings..."

"... Lord Nuffield has a marvellous scheme which I think is probably new since you were here...Any R.A.F. Crew can go to these Hostels at Nuffield's expense, plus 5 shillings per day for Sgts. and P.Os...."

"... The December Bloodstock sales were held last week at Newmarket. The highest price was for the two-year-old "Happy Landing", which fetched 2700 gns. Several others were sold for over 2000gns. each. It looks as though the buyers view the war situation as very satisfactory..."

"...Do you remember -----?...He was made a prisoner in Italy. When Italy was invaded he escaped to Switzerland. He is going to stay there and will continue his Medical studies at Lausanne University. Before doing this he is to tour the country, staying at all the best Hotels..."

"... Betty's Dive in York is now called the Oak Room. They think it is more dignified..."

"...The chap I was walking along the road with was asked if he was a Sgt Pilot. He blushed and answered, "No, but I hope to be one day"..."

Mail

Yesterday morning the two boxes that were left over from the day before were sorted and distributed They contained 1785 letters

At 11.00hrs. a further two boxes arrived. These contained 1413 letters which wre sorted and distributed during the afternoon.

There are still 7 boxes in transit.

A letter without an envelope has been received. The following are the particulars:
From: 30 Church Street, Hemel Hemstead, Herts.
To: My Dearest Brother, signed..Your Loving Sister, Puddy.
Claimants please see their postman.

German Radio

The German Radio last night reported that on the Beach-head of Nettuno the clearing-up of the area round Aprilia continued and the station of Aprilia was taken. Enemy attacks against the new German lines collapsed in the face of collective fire of all type of weapons. Since the landing the Americans and British have lost in the area of Nettuno over 4000 prisoners and 89 guns.

North American bomber formations flew in the midday hours of the 10th. Feb. with strong fighter protection, into the area of Central Germany.

The residential district of Brunswick was particularly hit. The German claim to have shot down 51 enemy aircraft, 32 being four-engined bombers.

American Graduates i

THE following is t and the "New York Herald a certain British Major w ican and British soldiers thods used by American Ga

New recruits receive th following address from th "little tubby man with sh eyes and irresistible la

"This is school of Murder. Murder is my busines Not the unclassified shooting at unknown persons in battle, but the personal, dividual murder of a man. It is an art which you ar learning - which you must practise and become effic in."

"The average Englishman and American is talented in fact born for this business, although at the beginning he may suffer a c tain amount from his cons ience!

"You must overcome this otherwise in a critical s uation it may cause your death. You must kill a J ry in the same way that y would squash a fly. Thin it over, and when you hav killed a few, you will sl like a baby even after th most bloody of slaughteri Only two things must inte est you - to experience i and come out of it"

This was followed by a description of the variou lessons taught in this school of the Major's. Th teaching of murder with a types of weapons, for ex ample shooting at automat puppets in dimly lighted

Record
CHRISTMAS.   Roll Call 9.00 & 3.00.   Saturday 12th. February 1944.

12

School of Murder

Gangsterism

rom the "Readers Digest"
e". The report is upon
ask it is to teach Amer-
special school, the me-
s.

ms, as well as the use of
ves and daggers.

The Major declares,
need men with cool pre-
ion - like the American
gster". He is an en-
siast of the typical Am-
can Gangster weapon -
automatic pistol. "One
s not shoot, but plays
s weapon", he says, "That
why it is called the
cago Piano; one must
rn the rhythm of it".

The "Volkischer Beobach-
" concluded this article
h the following comment:
warning can suffice a-
nst these criminals.
ir defeat is most necess-
in order that humane
an beings may exist".

OOTBALL COMMITTEE

A meeting of the Foot-
l Committee will be held
night at 7.00p.m. in the
en Barrack.
All Room representatives
asked to attend.

MENU

ll Camp - Stew.
----
ll Camp - Sausages or
Lamb Chops.

X-RAYS
Precautionary Measure

The whole Camp is to be
X-rayed. Some time ago we
asked for this and it was
promised at a Protecting
Power Conference and sub-
sequent conferences with the
Commandant. The Field Rad-
iography equipment has now
arrived at this Camp and the
German Authorities are making plans to X-ray every man
in the Camp.

The Medical Officers wel-
come this move as it gives
a chance for everyone in the
Camp to be X-rayed. As a
precautionary measure it will
be very beneficial as if any
disease is detected it may
be isolated immediately to
prevent its spreading to
other members of the Camp.

The X-rays are to start
on either Tuesday or Wed-
nesday.

Plans are being made to
X-ray by rooms and people
should see to it that they
are present when their room
is called up.

Brains Trust

The Scientific Discussion
Group will meet in D 12 on
Sunday between 3.15 and 4.15
pm. and 5.05 and 6.10pm.

Sgt. C.S. Dare will give
a talk on Dentistry and G.
Clayton one on Optics.

Musical Society

The Musical Society an-
nounces the usual gramophone
recital in the Theatre on
Sunday at 1.15 p.m.

WANTED

Will the Borrower please
return to BARRON B 7,
the following:
English Slide Rule:
Elementary Analysis.

On loan for a very
short period:
"Pamela" and "Clarissa"
by Samuel Richardson:
"Roderick Random" and
"Humphrey Clinker" by
Smollett.
Would anyone who poss-
esses any of these books
please bring them to:
J.A. JERMAN B 3.

French Society

There will be NO meet-
ing to-night. The first
meeting will be held at
7.15pm. on Saturday, 19th.
Feb. in the Green Barrack.
Thenceforward the Society
will meet every fortnight.

According to a Reuter
report, the U.S.A. Air
Force is to consist of
2,300,000 men. There will
be 100,799 pilots, 20,086
bomb aimer-gunners, 18,805
navigators, 107,218 gunners
, and 555,891 ground per-
sonnel and technicians.

weather

Max. — 1 deg. C.
Min. —1.4 deg. C.

To the Editor

Dear Sir, I would like
to take this opportunity
of thanking your paper and
the members of the compound
who took such great interest in the fate of my late
molar. I considered dis-
cretion to be the better
part of valour and Dr. Pol-
lock removed the offending
member. Hoping I shall be
favoured by a visit from
you, I am Yrs. Sin. C.Dare.

Printed and Published by
The MacAdam Press 22

Morale and Morality

Sitting in the editorial chair is, as the man said, better than working. And from our editorial chair we attempted to advise, chide (gently) and cajole our readers into using their Kriegie time to the best possible advantage, to equip themselves for the brave new future in the brave new Britain that the end of the war would bring. We believed, from the comfort of our chair, in leading from behind. (Some of our modern newspaper editorials give the impression that the leaders come from the behind.) So it was that in the third edition of the revived *Recco* we asked:

ARE YOU A JOE?
CIVILISATION TREMBLES

Deplorable as it is, the fact remains that the 'Not Joe' complex is easily the most noticeable trait of any prisoner of war who has been incarcerated for twelve months or more. Most Stalag inmates will agree that this is so. Who is or what is a "Joe"? The term is in the nature of a classification rather than a designation of any particular person. Anybody can be a "Joe", but there are some who are more vulnerable than others.

The typical "Joe" is always last when the blessings of life are handed out, and being last, he naturally stands an excellent chance of getting nothing at all. Conversely he usually collects a superabundance of anything that is to his disadvantage.

Good Reason

Now the prisoner has plenty of time to cogitate over the way of life, and, from observation of the above phenomena, he develops what is known in the German Stalags as the "Not Joe" complex or the determination not to be "Joe".

Obviously there must be a very good reason for this amazing change in outlook on the part of several thousands of tolerably well educated Britons. Many are the explanations which can be offered: bitterness, jealousy, mental instability, and the rest, but there is one that surely stands out above the rest. It is that of psychological reaction. Psychology, so the professors would have us believe, can explain all the vagaries of human nature and it is therefore reasonable to assume that the answer will be found in the matter of psychological reaction.

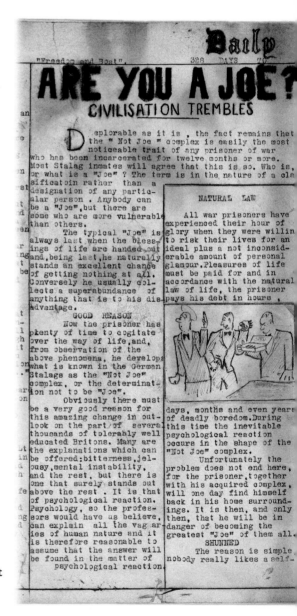

Natural Law

All war prisoners have experienced their hour of glory when they were willing to risk their lives for an ideal plus a not inconsiderable amount of personal glamour. Pleasures of life must be paid for and in accordance with the natural law of life, the prisoner pays his debt in hours, days, months and even years of deadly boredom. During this time the inevitable psychological reaction occurs in the shape of the Not Joe complex.

Unfortunately the problem does not end there, for the prisoner, together with his acquired complex, will one day find himself back in his home surroundings. It is then and only then, that he will be in danger of becoming the greatest Joe of them all.

Shunned

The reason is simple, nobody really likes a selfish person, and if the Not Joe continues to follow his prison life philosophy, he will very soon find himself in the unenviable position of a man found out and shunned by his friends.

A more sobering prospect cannot be imagined. So perhaps it might be as well to be Just Joe occasionally, just to preserve our civilised equilibrium.

That diatribe was followed just eleven days later by an even more hard-hitting attack on our fellow prisoners, or rather those amongst us who succumbed to the siren call of lethargy. We said:

ONE MANS MEAT

Have You Nothing To Do?

Recently we have seen a great number of new Kriegies, and what is more surprising a considerable number of old prisoners, wandering about day after day with a lost expression, and the complaint that they have nothing to do. With a newcomer who has not had time to find his feet nor accustom himself to the restriction of camp life, this is more or less understandable.

But how are we to regard an old lag who after 2 or 3 years internment has not found something with which to occupy his time and mind.

Around him his friends are busy studying. They study languages, economics, engineering ... practically every branch of life is covered.

If he is not keen to study, if he is content to go home with exactly the same amount of book learning that he had when he left, then there are other avenues of diversion. He can study art, music or if these subjects are beyond his scope and the stage attracts, there is a drama school for the veriest beginners.

There are many societies in the camp in which he can interest himself, societies both for amusement and for information.

If so inclined he can become a reporter for this paper, an undoubted honour and a very interesting occupation.

We note with regret this deplorable attitude of mingled apathy and cynicism which pervades the compound. We have no pity for the fellow who can find nothing to interest or amuse him. He is a poor weed, a parasite in a community which cannot afford to have parasites. Here of all places everyone must work as a body to help the body.

In the old days before the camp had an education committee A.D.S., societies, libraries, people said these things would never work. They are working now and you can take your part in them.

Now is the time to better your position. Here you have an unparalleled chance of study or variety. Preparation for lost war years should start now.

We place no faith in people who intend to begin their betterment once they are home. They are the procrastinators of our life, manana their motto.

Let your motto be Now.

A month later we returned to the subject, trying to encourage time-filling endeavour among our compatriots and at the same time, painting a revealing picture of the mental attitudes that affected us all – doers as well as dreamers.

THE LOTUS EATERS

How often do prisoners sit back and say Well, tomorrow I'll start to study? On the morrow, full of new life, happy with their new scheme, they rush madly around collecting books, paper and all the odds and ends of gen necessary for the opening of their new era. Ultimately they start to work, feverishly conning textbooks, writing essays, learning the theory of engines, sound and a thousand and one things.

Then after a few weeks comes the reaction. The student becomes more and more lethargic and the study periods less frequent. Instead of the feverish every-day activity, he spends odd days at his work, seeking, in simple excuses, relief from his self-imposed task. Ultimately his books lie unused. He retires to his bed again saying Well, I didn't want to be a B.Sc. anyway.

Every day prisoners lie on their beds and make up their minds to do something new on the morrow.

They take it up, work madly for a few weeks then throw the whole idea over. Some say it is a confession of weakness on the part of the prisoner, vacillation, lack of power to make up his mind. Perhaps this is so.

But possibly the greatest factor in this lack of staying-power of the average prisoner is the complete unsettledness of his mind. We have no guarantee of what tomorrow will bring. In actual fact it will probably be exactly the same as today – as monotonous as hell – but lurking at the back of every prisoner's mind is the vain hope that something startling and different will happen – invasion, a smashing development in the war which drags interminably, some cataclysmic upheaval, something exciting.

This is the real reason why he cannot apply himself to one set thing for a prolonged period of time. Despite the monotony of this life from day to day, the average prisoner is in a constant state of mental turmoil. His mind wanders off into a utopian state which he knows as home and which he has probably not seen for three or more years.

Although he tries desperately to fill his time as usefully as possible, to study, to add to his knowledge, this constant state of waiting for what he does not know, saps his power of concentration until, if he is not very careful, he will end up as an idle and useless dreamer. Not a bad life, but hardly one calculated to improve one's position in future life . . .

The camp reaction to our little homilies must have been rewarding because from the editorial chair, now beginning in some minds to look more like a pulpit, we again, risking our own life and limb in the process, castigated our fellow prisoners.

FOOLS' PARADISE
RE-ADJUSTMENT OF IDEAS NECESSARY

Men confined react to their imprisonment in a variety of ways. The unholy deadness of prison life breeds the introverts and the neurotics, the perverts and the grafters. Whether it will breed the congenital idiots of our future cities is still to be seen.

Certainly we revel in the suggestion of mental unbalance. We venerate the excesses of the pixilated, even condone them. The Pathans have a similar custom, but in the progressive cities of never-never land such barbaric beliefs are neither encouraged nor tolerated. The aimless are suspect and the half-witted detained at the pleasure and expense of the estate.

Think ... sterilisation and detention are the rewards of lightly-cultivated imbecility.

Megalomania is a prevalent stalag relaxation, but it has all the fundamentals of a dangerous hobby.

The prisoner has time to dream fabulous dreams.

They become watertight propositions; multiple combines dance tantalisingly on the solid foundation of Air Force back pay. Wall Street is rocked from these same humble sources. West End audiences cling to their seats, a new personality sweeps the stage ... perhaps the choice of words is not fortunate . But this state of mind is ludicrously pathetic.

Do not forget that those two great megalomaniacs Horatio Bottomley and Leopold Harris got twenty years on a capital investment of personality plus and a few odd millions.

Plainly ... no matter how much we are imbued with admiration for these present conditions of subnormal understanding, we must appreciate that there is no room in the modern state for the simpering pervert, the slap-happy stalag speculator nor the mock-pitiful Kriegsgefangener who is prepared to lick four years' wounds for forty more. These are mental cultures of a useless existence from which there is little to salvage.

The respective merits are few, but we can face the future with an ox-like patience bred in adversity.

We have existed in hovels, eaten like animals and been subjected to humiliation.

As POWs our position might have been inconceivably worse, but as citizens there is no strata of the state which will demand so much forbearance of us. At least we are hardened to stand the trials which may confront us on our return, but the future surely depends on the individual's ability to discard acquired habits ... painstakingly transformed into unimpeachable customs.

But all our editorials weren't such heavy stuff. And we got just as much reaction from our lighter pieces as from the homilies. Just after we published *One Man's Meat* exhorting our fellow Kriegies to get up and going, we received a letter from a reader who had been stirred from his lethargy long enough to put pen to paper. We read the letter and gave the matter some further thought . . . and managed to fill a few more columns in the *Recco*:

ANOTHER MAN'S POISON

Following our article One mans' meat, we have reconsidered the problem and have reached, with the help of Readers Digest, the following conclusions:

From childhood we hear our elders talk about lazy people as if laziness were ignoble, whereas the truth is that except for our lazy men there would be no progress.

When a little girl helping her mother to clear away the dinner dishes sensibly carries a large tray-load to eliminate more journeys, the mother chidingly says lazy man's load. After a few such observations the child, by the time she is grown up, wears the world-weary expression so common to housewives who imagine that laziness is a curse. Most women, it may be noticed, show their age sooner than men, doubtless because the average woman is less lazy than her husband.

The lazy waiter in a restaurant is always the most satisfactory and best. He brings everything the diner will need on the first trip because he regards every extra step as an abomination.

Nearly all progress in human affairs must have been due to the contriving of lazy men to save themselves steps. The first boat – a hollow log – must have been born of the desire of one of our ancestors to avoid walking round a lake or along the bank of a river.

Inventors often devise labour-saving devices that they themselves would have no occasion to use.

They sell them, and the money thus made enables them to live without working so hard. Thus it is that laziness is the urge to the inventive effort.

Many of our greatest statesmen were brought up on farms and would have remained on farms if they hadn't been too lazy to face so much work.

It is time that we lazy people were receiving the serious consideration that is our due. We comprise the hope of our race.

The complete about-face in editorial policy brought us instant friends. The loafers, lay-abouts and pit-dwellers smiled smugly as they continued to coast through the days and nights of incarceration . . . they had been right all along. They were the thinkers saving themselves – and us – for a glorious future. They were glad that they had taken the trouble to get out of bed to read that morning's edition of the *Recco*.

On February 26 (304 days to Christmas) we carried a letter from a bunch of characters who had been made merry – and thoughtful – by one of the infrequent home-brews that Kriegies managed to make from dried fruit sent to the camp in bulk by, among others, Sir Knatchbull-Hugessen, the British Ambassador in Turkey whose safe, we learned later, was frequently opened and its state secrets rifled, by his Lordship's manservant, code-name Cicero. The brews were sometimes condoned by the Germans who took the view that they kept us out of other mischief. Sometimes they were banned when the prisoners became too belligerent or when, as happened once, some of the prisoners became temporarily blind as the galvanising from the pail in which the brew had been made, caused this most unexpected and dangerous reaction.

A refinement to the simple raisin, date and fig wines that were produced was the distillation of the mash at the end of the brewing process. This was achieved by hammering and rolling tins into thin tubes whose edges were sealed with the solder melted from the tops of the tins of 50 cigarettes which came to us through either the Red Cross or personal parcels from home. The pencil-thin tubes were wrapped in wet cloth to condense the steam passing through them from the boiling mash below. The drops of liquid fire were then gathered in another tin. The raw spirit, and the word raw is used advisedly, was then mixed with the wine to fortify it – and the drinkers. A few hardy souls were known to drink the spirit raw – with a variety of effects.

It appears that the brew quaffed by our friends on the night of February 25, 1944, was of the type that bred brotherly love and compassion:

Letter to the Editor

A party of men who had been partaking of the blood of the raisin entered our office yesterday and presented us with the following letter. We feel confident that you will be interested.

Dear Sir

We the undersigned frown upon the older Kriegies who wait at the wire for the arrival of new prisoners who have (God bless 'em) been issued with a windbreaker at Dulag. These older Kriegies (the robbing b . . . . . .s) endeavour to trade their worn battledress tunics for the aforementioned windbreakers and then strut smugly round the blasted compound Yours

C. Hubbett

R. Cartwright

G. Lewis

A. Macaskill

The above gentlemen also lodged a complaint that WOs and other ranks had to use the same latrine.

Ignoring the frivolous complaint from the recently-promoted Warrant Officers (but it did make a difference to our back-pay once we got home to Blighty) we followed up the letter in our issue of February 28.

Fleecing the Innocents

In view of the jocular and favourable comment aroused by Saturday's letter to the Editor, we have confirmation that the old Stalag sport of rooking the new prisoner is looked upon with general disfavour.

Certain of our leading sportsmen have a peculiar talent for watching them coming up the home stretch and picking a cert. winner 20 lengths from the post.

At first this talent appears to be a remarkable one akin to second sight or Ouija-board manipulation.

Captain Victor – the world-famous *Daily Recco* correspondent – wholeheartedly refutes this point of view and, in the interests of fair play, offers the following advice: 'Your choice should be well shod, heavy in coat, and a five day journey in horse trucks is no disadvantage.

'A heavily weighted young 'un offers more than a good 'un carrying less poundage, as the latter type are inclined to be intractable. That dazed and hungry look should also be considered as a favourable omen.

'Groom your choice well for a couple of days, then clip coat and shoe in lighter fashion for the midsummer sprints. Even in midwinter one has to look ahead,' adds Captain Victor.

Further to this – in the interests of a sporting flutter – our correspondent challenges all comers, laying 50 Rothmans against an Irwin Jacket (good condition) that, from the next list of the above have arrived he will make a selection and have it completely shorn and shoeless within 50 yards.

Frankly older and wiser prisoners who now view with revulsion the exploitation indulged in by smooth-talking dulagian hucksters, feel that this fleecing of the innocents should be discouraged.

It is sheer hypocrisy to condemn the favoured few, if we harbour in our midst disciples of their policy.

The enforced inactivity, the perpetual sameness, the ever present wire which enclosed not just the camp but our minds as well, the utter boredom, the constant waiting for Christmas and the desperate need to know how the war was progressing, bred rumours like the flies which made summer in camp an itchy misery. On February 22 (308 days to Christmas) we tried to warn our fellow Kriegies about the dangers of having too many too often:

Did You Start it?
10% of Rumours Are True
I got it from Ted. You know he doesn't spread duff gen.

How often have you heard that sentence, muttered furtively in a corner, or said openly in a crowd, since you have been a prisoner? Rumour, rumour, rumour, every day the camp seethes like a teeming ant-bed with rumour.

The man who said that without rumours a Kriegie would go mad was undoubtedly right. A good strong rumour drags the average Kriegie from his normally lethargic state and drives him around to see his friends just to see if they have heard …

Where do rumours come from? Careful analysis has proved that they spring from the following sources 40% are wishful thinking out loud

30% are wrong interpretations of things just overheard

20% are maliciously started

10% are ultimately proved true.

Rumours are a god-send to the wire-weary Kriegie suffering from an enforced inferiority complex; it gives him a great kick to give his fellows first-hand information.

Came from a posten in the cooler, the truth, boy ... his ego is inflated by being able to give what appears to be first-hand information, even if he knows it is unreliable, or even untrue.

Then again, how often has Turkey been in the war? Countless times and all because someone rolled over on his pit and said to his neighbour if Turkey was in the war we'd win in 8 weeks.

Further down the barrack someone catches the Turkey and the war and so a first-class rumour starts.

Wherever they start and however they end, rumours are an undoubted source of amusement.

Tracking them down keeps many people from going round the bend. Listening to them provides much food for thought.

But we deplore the large number of entirely unfounded rumours which have been floating round this camp during the last few weeks.

By the way, have you heard ...?

Departures & Arrivals

The most distressing news we ever had to print was published on the morning of Friday, April 21, 1944.

47 OFFICERS KILLED
GERMAN STATEMENT

Following numerous requests that the notice which was read out by the Germans on the evening roll-call of Wednesday 19th, be published, we have incorporated it in our columns.

"During the course of re-capturing RAF Officers following a mass escape, some officers offered resistance to arrest. Others, after being re-caught, made renewed attempts to escape during the journey back to the camp.

In the above mentioned cases force of arms had to be resorted to, with the result that 47 prisoners of war were shot and killed."

There it was in black and white. Now everyone in the camp believed it.

We had, of course, heard about the mass and ill-fated escape attempt at our former camp in Sagan. And we had heard that some of the officers had been shot. The camp, as never before, buzzed with rumours. In agreement with Dixie we decided not to publish anything – there was enough gloom, despondency and hatred circulating without the *Recco* adding fuel to the flames. But the German version of the escape and the shootings was so obscene that no-one could believe it. We knew that, in the past when escape attempts had gone wrong, the unlucky capturees were roughed up by the guards . . . that was one of the risks. We also knew that with an escape bungled and detected, there was no way that the prisoners would create any kind of risk or danger to their captors. It was always a case of bad luck, better luck next time.

The fateful attempt by the officers was made at a time when tension between prisoners and guards was high in all camps. There had been numerous incidents and countless cases of reprisals taken by the Kommandantur in our own collection of compounds. The *Recco* had been banned for a twelve day stretch and was now appearing only under censorship. Inter compound sports events had been cancelled without

The *Daily Recco* of Friday April 21, 1944 carried one of the most distressing headlines – news of the shooting of 47 fellow POWs and RAF officers after an escape attempt from the camp at Sagan

Issue no 62

Daily Recco

"Freedom and Recce"   Roll Calls 0800 and 1600   Friday 21st April 1944

German Radio

The German radio last night reported that:
"Before noon yesterday formations of American bombers carried out raids on W. and C. Germany. Damage and casualties resulted in KASSEL and PADERBORN. 31 a/c were shot down, most of these were 4-engined bombers.

American a/c sank the Swedish ship ENDLA off the S. coast of France.

Last night light German bombers raided targets in the LONDON area.

The Rumanian communique reports heavy fighting round PASCANI.

N.E. of SEBASTOPOL Soviet attacks were again repulsed and a large number of tanks destroyed. In air battles 56 Soviet a/c were destroyed and a further 20 were damaged on the ground.

In the Lower DNIESTER area German forces won a defensive success on both sides of the TIGHINA.

Between the CARPATHIANS and the Upper DNIESTER German and Hungarian forces smashed Soviet resistance and threw the enemy further back. Soviet counter-attacks were repulsed.

Behind the German lines in the Central sector German forces have been engaged in fighting enemy bands. Over 1000 bandits were killed and more 100 encampments destroyed.

S.W. of NARWA German troops penetrated Soviet positions despite strong resistance and inflicted high losses. 30 guns were destroyed.

In Italy an enemy thrust on the NETTUNO beach-head N.W. of LITTORIA collapsed against the strong defensive fire of the German positions.

47 Officers Killed

German Statement

Following numerous requests that the notice which read out by the Germans on the evening roll-call of Wednesday 19th., be published, we have incorporated it in our columns.

"During the course of re-capturing R.A.F. officers following a mass escape, some officers offered resistance to arrest. Others after being re-caught, made renewed attempts to escape during the journey back to the camp.

In the above mentioned cases force of arms had to be resorted to, with the result that 47 prisoners of war were shot and killed."

World Press News

The Australian War Minister, Mr. Francis Ford, drew British and American attention to the fact that Australia must have a 30 million population in 30 years' time instead of the 7 million of to-day. Australia must be populated or it would be lost.

The "Leader" commenting on Maisky's biography, says "Any Englishman reading it would be so shocked that it would be a long while before he would believe any Govt. statesman or paper again."

Raffle

The raffle for pyjamas and cardigan was won by DEWAR A 3.

Motor Sports Club

The above club will meet in the small tent this evening at 5.30.
The speaker will be "Pop" Haycock.

M E N U

All Camp – German meat stew
B 5 6 & 7 – German steaks.

A B & C – Cold corned mutton & potatoes.
D Block – Fritters.

Will anyone who has a Penguin copy of "The Loom of Youth" by A. Waugh, see WESTON C 11.

Wanted

Wanted cigarettes for one pair of black shoes size 9 one shirt and one pair of khaki shorts.
MARTYN   A 13.

Wanted a pair of new shorts for a set of summer underwear.
Brady   D 3.

Wanted cigarettes for American windsheeter.
SNOOK   B 8.

Wanted cigarettes (50 for 2 ounces) for St. Julien pipe tobacco.
GREEN   D 5.

Wanted cigarettes for American leather jacket.
SWITZER   B 4.

Wanted boot polish for cigarettes.
CRITCHETT   C 5.

Wanted drying cloths for cigarettes.
MURRAY   B 9.

MACKAY WHITLOCK
PRESS

warning and other camp activities restricted to the point of extinction. The trouble was not hard to find. The Allied campaign was reaching a crescendo. The might of the Third and Glorious Reich was on the wane. Japes and practical jokes played by the prisoners on the guards which had previously been met with a guffaw, an oath or at worst a shove from the victim, were now met by a quick march to the cooler or a jab with a rifle butt.

At the start of our captivity our guards had been a mixture of young and middle-aged Germans, many of them regular soldiers and similar in dedication and intelligence to soldiers anywhere. On their side they had feats of arms and wide ranging victories which looked as if they would never end. The guards were a mixture of boastfulness and the generosity that a powerful victor can show to a defeated and inferior enemy.

Then, for a time, we had older men as guards, men who had been called from their civilian occupations to help the Fatherland when the Blitzkriegs ran out of blitz. They were delighted to talk to the prisoners, to talk about the civvy street jobs they were dying to get back to, to tell us, again and again, that they wanted no part of any war, that, like us, they were praying for it to end.

They were soon replaced by a much younger, tougher breed of guard. These men had seen service and been wounded on the Russian front. The bitterness of their continuing defeats at the hands of Ivan obviously rankled. The prisoners were fair – and easy – game. This was the worst time of our captivity, made even worse later when Red Cross supplies became short and sometimes nonexistent. It was such guards that met the officers as they crawled out of their tunnel. The officers, bewildered and dazzled by searchlights, stood no chance. In our compound hatred was a palpable thing.

The shooting of the officers culminated a period of worsening relations between prisoners and guards. A further possible reason for the trouble on the German side was the fact that the Luftwaffe was finding it increasingly difficult to cope with the hundreds of Allied prisoners who were being shot down each week as the number of night and daylight raids on the heart of Germany grew in volume.

On Wednesday March 1, 1944 we had told our readers that following a conference with the Commandant, the camp was due to build up to 8000 prisoners (see extract of this issue on page 80/81). A few issues later we gave the camp the latest information on the new arrivals, plus a few titbits of local gossip. (See opposite)

Reeed

+++   +++

HARRY'S
BUSTER

+++   +++

See Notices for Details.

George Potter Leaves

Gunner G.Potter N.Z.E.F.
alias George Pape, whose
change-over was detected,
was taken back to Lamsdorf
at the week-end. He wishes
to thank the Compound for
the co-operation he re-
ceived during the two
years he was with us.

Chess Solution

Key move:
1. Q-Q5, any move.
2. B-B3, any move.
then 3. QxR, Q-R8, Q-Kt.8
or Q-R2. MATE.

The Protecting Power
will visit this Camp on
Friday 10th. March.

Red Cross

An issue of Matches
will be made in the near
future.
A party is going to the
Station this morning.

Competition

Cigarettes from advt.
fees this week will go
to the person who brings
us the week's best item
of Mail Gen.
Last week's competit-
ion was won by W/O W.H.
Butcher   B5 who handed
in the best Line.

The evening meals will
in future be served im-
mediately after roll call.

E Lager is in urgent
need of old vests and
pants for sports wear.
Contributions to J.Bryce
B 9.

News from Newcomers
From Our Special Correspondent

Compound strength in E Lager is now 1416 men -
approximately 852 of these are U.S.A.F.   Underneath
we publish a few of the highlights from this Lager.

NEW   ARRIVALS

A party of 120 arrived
yesterday, of these 101
were U.S.A.F. and the re-
mainder British. On the
journey from Dulag two men
escaped - one was recaptured
but the other is still a-
drift. They brought news
of a new R.A.F. Camp at
Marienburg.

"LONDON BLITZED"

One of the new arrivals
who was in London during the
1000 a/c raid, said, "No-one
even got out of bed. The
Germans dropped hundreds of
flares and lit up the whole
city like day. A few bombs
were dropped on the fringes
of S.London".

NEW SWING BAND

There is plenty of talent
in E Lager for a swing band
which is now under way.
Band-leader Larry Press, himself an Ace Drummer, has
figured several times in
"Down Beat", the American
Swing Monthly. In 1940 he
made a $21000 tour with his
Band.

ANOTHER FORECAST

Two rival prophets have
sprung up in the new Lager.
One, an old established
seer, with a long line of
past successes forecast the
end of the war on April 15th
The other, who is having
trouble with his Spirits,
has not yet got a line on
"The Big Date". At present

by his own secret system he
is able, by inspecting the
back of your neck to tell
your name, Home town, married
or single and how many children. He is training his
"Spirits" up for the Invasion
Stakes.

POLISH AMAZONS

A new arrival stated that
several Battalions of Polish
Women Volunteer Troops are
in training in England.
Pictures ahve already
appeared in National Newspapers of these Amazons in
Bayonet Charges.

NOT SO GREEN

Ex-A-Lagerites who went
to E Lager for a change from
sand to grass are disappointed
because it has disappeared in
a Sea of Mud.

ROB ROY

Sgt. R.R.Mackenzie Graham
who is organising the new
Theatre, has had several arguments with Exalted Person-
ages in Grey Uniforms.

TAIL-PIECE

NEWBOY (on being given
his 50 cigarettes for the week)
"I suppose this is the regular German Issue?".
(Collapse of several well-
known Red Cross Kings.)

Wanted urgently by the
Theatre - coloured civilian
neck-ties on loan. Please
hand to Lacharité A 7.

Continuing our education theme we decided to help the many new Kriegies in the camp by giving them a short lesson in what was probably the camp's most-used word – Gash. Or maybe it was just the most used non-swear word:

GOT ANY GASH? GOT ANY GASH? WHAT IS GASH . . .

Gash is surely one of the most expressive words in the Kriegie vocabulary. Originally we believe, it was a word used exclusively in the navy and merchant marine – the name given to the chute through which all waste, slops, etc, were precipitated into Davy Jones Locker – the gash chute being an essential part of any vessel.

Now, gash is probably the most-used word in this camp. Anything is, or can be, gash – food, brews, books or coal.

Got any gash? is the Kriegie cry throughout the length and breadth of Germany, an expressive request for anything from a rotten swede to a pair of boots.

Even the Kriegie himself tends to gashness standing by the fire or lying on his pit, just staring into space dreaming of better days to come, he will lugubriously exclaim Hell – I'm gash.

When all this is over and we are standing in some pub, sucking in a triple whisky bought with the last of our back pay, we won't be at all surprised to hear a plaintive voice enquire Got any gash here?

The pressure on the Germans – and consequently on us – was highlighted in our issue of March 9 when we told the horrified camp that *lebensraum* was so tight that tents were to be erected in the compound.

NEW PRISONERS TO GO UNDER CANVAS
TENTS ON SPORTSFIELD ANSWER TO SPORTS SPACE PLEA

At the conference with the Kommandant held yesterday in the Vorlager, main business under discussion was points to be raised at the protecting power meeting on Friday.

In a short time the strength of the existing three compounds may be brought up to 9,000 prisoners.

This bombshell hit Sgt. Deans, Sgt. Mogg and the leaders of 2 and 3 compounds when at the conference Sgt Deans was requesting more room for sportsfields.

The Kommandant stated that the extra men would have to be accommodated wherever possible. Five tents, each capable of holding 500 men, would be provided.

The Kommandant added that all recreational space would have to be used for the erection of tents to accommodate new prisoners.

This matter is to be brought up before the protecting power on Friday.

And on Monday March 13 we devoted much of the *Recco* to giving details of that all-important meeting. The Kriegies jostled and queued for hours to read all about it.

PROTECTING POWER VISIT

Attaché Msr W Braun and Secretary Msr Wagner, representatives of the protecting power, visited the camp on Friday March 10. A conference was held with Sgts. Deans, Mogg, Lunsford and Clarke.

The attaché was told that Polish and Czech POWs had arrived recently at the camp.

The attaché referred to the stripping of NCOs during Gestapo searches. He stated that the Kommandant could not be held responsible and that the special police were empowered to carry out periodic searches of prisoners. Such searches must be carried out in a decent manner – the P.P. to be informed if this was not done and they would do all possible to see that searches were carried out in accordance with the Geneva Convention.

The attaché promised to take up the matter of the lack of accommodation in the sick bay with the commandant and High Command. The doctors informed the attaché of the shortage of dressings and asked for two more Doctors and a Dental Officer. The attaché had no knowledge of the coming of the next medical Commission but promised to enquire.

Msr Braun promised to press for action in the matter of the transfer of Dominion and Colonial prisoners to warmer climates.

Sgt. Deans requested a scale of treatment for NCOs in arrest and the attaché said he would try to secure it.

The point regarding Court Martial for damage to German property was discussed; the attaché said that men would not be liable to Courts Martial for such trivial acts as cutting the wire in attempt to escape – on the other hand if prisoners took Reich property with them on escapes they would then be liable to such a charge.

Msr Braun promised to enquire into the Censoring at Sagan, to speed up mail delivery and to look into the matter of facilities for Telegrams to Next-of-Kin. He said that he had asked for an RC padre to be sent here as soon as possible.

General shortage of cooking equipment was brought up. It was stated that the position would be bad when the camp increased to 9,000. Msr Braun promised to take up the matter and commented that he was glad to see the communal cooking of Red Cross food in this camp as it was by far the most economical and efficient way of dealing with it. Sgt. Deans said that might be so if cooking facilities were adequate. The Attaché also promised to look into the matter of fresh vegetables.

After a request that shutters, on both sides of the hut should be permitted to be left open after lights out, the attaché said he would talk with the Commandant.

There was considerable discussion about the supply and storage of Red Cross food reserves. Sgt. Deans said that the present storage facilities were inadequate and would be even worse with an increase to 9000 men when a reserve of 100000 parcels would be required. At present camp strength the reserve was only 7 weeks duration and the number of prisoners was increasing daily. Msr Braun said that he would see the RC as soon as possible. Sgt. Deans said that he had already telegraphed them.

The attaché said he would look into the matter of the lack of clothing repair facilities.

He promised to try to obtain for the prisoners a copy of the official scale of rations issued by the German authorities.

Sgt. Deans complained of the lack of recreation space which was bad already and when the Sportsfields were used for tents the conditions would be even worse. Msr Braun stated that he and the Kommandant were of the same opinion as Sgt. Deans; He promised to report the matter of the overcrowding in the barracks. Sgt. Deans suggested that organised walks should be permitted – these were essential to the health of the camp if sports facilities were not possible.

The overcrowding, with dropping morale as a side-effect, was already being experienced in the camp. In a call to brushes to prevent any further slippage and the possibility of disease, we wrote on March 16:

THE SLUM DWELLERS
WILL YOUR BARRACK WIN THE GONG?

Contrary to appearance, there is no authorised rubbish tip immediately outside any barrack in this compound.

The individuals who, deliberately or by negligence, leave refuse strewn about before their doors and windows for days on end, not only make the compound more hideous than it naturally is, but also create unnecessary work for the duty barracks. Every week at least twenty men are required to work picking up paper, boxes, tins, rags, ashes and generally cleaning up the mess around other people's doorsteps.

A certain amount of unnecessary work is also caused by the carelessness of Duty Stooges who empty their rubbish around, instead of into, the dust cart; but this is a minor nuisance compared with that arising from the general slovenliness mentioned above.

There are some barracks that regularly contribute more than their fair share of communal dirt for the communal worker to clean up. Their occupants come near to qualifying for the title of nature's slum dwellers; showing a perseverance in the creation of squalor that, in almost any other cause, would be praiseworthy. We understand moreover that these slumdwellers do not show any more than average enthusiasm for the communal cleaning work – of which they are so largely the cause – when it is their turn to be duty block.

The Duty Fuhrer has observed this state of affairs and, feeling that something should be done about it – other than mere exhortation – has arranged, regardless of expense, to present each week to the barrack which distinguishes itself by the dirtiness of its surroundings, a decoration or distinctive order.

This decoration will be knows as The Order of the Crumby Crest (crossed muckrakes rampant on a field brun).

This award will be made each week by impartial judges, who will take into consideration reports made by duty barracks and others concerned with camp cleanliness. The judges' decision will be final.

The name of the winning barrack will be published in these columns next week.

Camp humour

The following pages show a run of nine issues of the *Daily Recco* between March 6 and March 15, 1944.

Daily
"Freedor
295 D.

M.B. Splitters

"...Darling in your letters you must not say that after the war you'll probably put yourself out to stud it is'nt nice..."

"... There has been a half hour programme on the radio broadcast to America featuring Stalag 8B Band again and stories from repatriated prisoners most of them told by the men themselves . On the whole they were cheerful happy stories, but they made us think . The one unhappy one was told by a man who came home and found his wife and child had been killed in a Blitz and the most serious one was told by a girl ambulance driver who had been captured and who had nursed in P.O.W. hospitals. She spoke of the splendid spirit of comradship that captivity engendered..."

"... Went to the Guild Hall to see the Stalingrad Sword a marvellous piece of craftsmanship to be presented by us to Russia in Gold and Silver .Hand made by a craftsman now in the R.A.F...."

"... Miss..... has just had another baby. I dont know what the place is coming to.

Sgt. Deans has now been granted a permanent pass by the Germans . This pass enables him to go to both 2 & 3 Lagers and into the Vorlager up to the time that the Red Line comes into operation . The Camp Leader has also to wear a white armband to enable postens to recognise him easily .

Fools' Paradise

Re-adjustment of Ideas Necessary

Men canfined react to their imprisonment in a variety of ways . The unholy deadness of prison life breeds the introverts and the neurotics , the perver and the grafters . Whether it will breed the congeni idiots of our future cities has still to be seen .

Certainly we revel in the suggestion of " Mental Unbalance ". We venerate the excesses of the pixilated , even condone them . The Pathans have a similar custom , but in the progressive cities of Never-Never Land such barbaric beliefs are neither encouraged nor tolerated; the aimless are suspect and the half-witted detained at the pleasure and expense of the State .

Think...sterilisation and detention are the rewards for lightly cultivated imbaciliy .

Megalomania is a prevalent Stalag relaxation , but it has all the fundamentals of a dangerous hobby. The prisoner has time to dream fabulous dreams . They become watertight propositions ; multiple combines dance tantalizing on the solid foundations of Air Force back pay. Wall Street is rocked from the same humble source . West End audiences cling to their seats as a new personality sweeps the stage-- perhaps the choise of words is not fortunate-- but this state of mind is ludicrously pathetic.

Do not forget that those two great megalomaniacs Horatio Bottomley and Leopold Harris got twenty years on a capital investment of personality plus and a few odd millions .

Plainly-- no matter h much we are imbued with admiration for these pre ent conditions of subnor understanding , we must appreciate that there is no room in the modern st for the simpering perver the slap-happy Stalag sp ulator nor the mock piti Kriegsgefangener who is prepared to lick four ye wounds for forty more. These are mental culture of a useless existence from which there is litt to salvage.

The respective merits are few, but we can face the future with an ox-li patience bred in adversi We have existed in hovel eaten like animals amd b subjected to humiliation

As P.O.W's, our posit might have been inconcei ably worse, but as citiz there is no strata of the State which will dem and so much forbearance us. At least we are hard ened to stand the trials which may confront us on our return, but the futu surely depends on the in ividuals ability to disc acquired habits-- pains takingly transformed int unimpeachable customs .

Recently two lamp fit tings were removed from Green Hut . There have b in the past several case of fittings and wire bei stolen from the latrines This is an anti-social c You can stop it.

d Boat"
hristmas

Roll Call 0900 and 1600 Monday 6th March 1944

++   +++

HARRY'S
BUSTER

+++   +++

e Notices for Details.

eorge Potter Leaves

Gunner G.Potter N.Z.E.F.
as George Pape, whose
ange-over was detected,
s taken back to Lamsdorf
the week-end. He wishes
thank the Compound for
e co-operation he re-
ived during the two
ars he was with us.

Chess Solution

ey move:
Q-Q5, any move.
B-B3, any move.
en 3. QxR, Q-R8, Q-Kt.8
Q-R2. MATE.

The Protecting Power
ll visit this Camp on
iday 10th. March.

Red Cross

An issue of Matches
ll be made in the near
ture.
A party is going to the
ation this morning.

Competition

Cigarettes from advt.
es this week will go
the person who brings
the week's best item
Mail Gen.
Last week's competit-
n was won by W/O W.H.
tcher B5 who handed
the best Line.

The evening meals will
future be served im-
diately after roll call

E Lager is in urgent
ed of old vests and
nts for sports wear.
ontributions to J.Bryce
9.

News from Newcomers
From Our Special Correspondent

Compound strength in E Lager is now 1416 men –
approximately 852 of these are U.S.A.F.   Underneath
we publish a few of the highlights from this Lager.

NEW   ARRIVALS

A party of 120 arrived
yesterday, of these 101
were U.S.A.A.F. and the remainder British. On the
journey from Dulag two men
escaped – one was recaptured
but the other is still a-
drift. They brought news
of a new R.A.F. Camp at
Marienburg.

"LONDON   BLITZED"

One of the new arrivals
who was in London during the
1000 a/c raid, said, "No-one
even got out of bed. The
Germans dropped hundreds of
flares and lit up the whole
city like day. A few bombs
were dropped on the fringes
of S.London".

NEW SWING BAND

There is plenty of talent
in E Lager for a swing band
which is now under way.
Band-leader Larry Press, himself an Ace Drummer, has
figured several times in
"Down Beat", the American
Swing Monthly. In 1940 he
made a £21000 tour with his
Band.

ANOTHER FORECAST

Two rival prophets have
sprung up in the new Lager.
One, an old established
seer, with a long line of
past successes forecast the
end of the war on April 15th
The other, who is having
trouble with his Spirits,
has not yet got a line on
"The Big Date".   At present

by his own secret system he
is able, by inspecting the
back of your neck to tell
your name, Home town, married
or single and how many children. He is training his
"Spirits" up for the Invasion
Stakes.

POLISH AMAZONS

A new arrival stated that
several Battalions of Polish
Women Volunteer Troops are
in training in England.
Pictures ahve already
appeared in National Newspapers of these Amazons in
Bayonet Charges.

NOT SO GREEN

Ex-A-Lagerites who went
to E Lager for a change from
sand to grass are disappointed
because it has disappeared in
a Sea of Mud.

ROB ROY

Sgt. R.R.Mackenzie Graham
who is organising the new
Theatre, has had several arguments with Exalted Person-
ages in Grey Uniforms.

TAIL-PIECE

NEWBOY (on being given
his 50 cigarettes for the week)
"I suppose this is the regular German Issue?".
(Collapse of several well-
known Red Cross Kings.)

Wanted urgently by the
Theatre – coloured civilian
neck-ties on loan. Please
hand to Lacharité A 7.

Daily
"Freedom"
294 Days

M.B. Splitters

"... We have read a lot about your camp in a Red Cross magazine . You seem to have some interesting people there , is it really true that you have a swimming pool there because we have heard so ..."

The following letter is from a Kriegie in an Army camp to a P.O.W. in this camp.

"...I have not heard from you for some time , only one letter so far and that from England . I hope to see you in due course but I hear that Sgts. and Privates are not allowed together , anyhow you might be a Bloody General by then....This year, next year, sometime , never should see the end of the war . Hope all is well with you and yours I am about the same internally, externally I have a protruding gut a bald head and am almost toothless...
...Aufweideshen Uncle...."

"...Written by a dear old lady to Lord Woolton when Minister for Food,
'You have fed us in a wonderful way My Lord , I cant eat the bacon or cheese--- but that is the fault of my stomach, not Your Lordship's'..."

" ...Glad to hear that your wounds are healed O.K. ....wish I had been there to hold your hand during the operation , would I have promised not to look? ...no , on second thoughts I dont think I would have liked to see it..."

"....One woman talking to her friend...'I am so worried about Walter going round with a Jeep 'dont worry a Jeep is a female Jap....."

Scapa Flow
A Footnote to History

After the Arimstice the German fleet of about 70 warships lay interned at Scapa Flow . While their fate was being decided by the Allies at Versailles , Rear Admiral Von Reuter laid plans to sink the ships rather than surrender them . On June 17 th. 1919 he despatched th the officers this secret message : " Make preparations for the immediate scuttling of all ships , (I) if the British attempt to seize them by numbers (2) upon recept of the code signal , para acknowledge .

On June 2I st. British Admiral Sydney Freemantle took his fleet to sea for torpedo pracitde . Only 7 trawlers and 2 destroyers were left to guard the German fleet that morning when Von Reuter received news that the Versailles Conference had rejected Germany's proposals . " Make the signal " he ordered his Chief of Staff " Para 2 Acknowledge ".

Bright pennants fluttered in the sunshine and immediately on each of the ships officers opened the seacocks and began to abandon ship . Unaware of what was taking place, a party of school children watched the activity from a near-by steamer .

A London artist on a guarding trawler was the first to give the alarm . It was almost noon when he noticed that the Kaiser Friedrich Der Grosse, which he was sketching , was settling in the water, the boats were being lowered and she had raised the Ready For Battle pennant . Radio messages were flashed to the British Fleet .Men on the trawlers attempted to make the unwilling German sailors go back and close the valves . Rifle shots rang out : I3 Germans were killed and a score wounded The British managed to beach several destroyers but could do little with the big ships .

Shortly after mid-day the Kaiser Friedrich Der Grosse turned over and sank : I5 more had gone by the time Admiral Freemantle's ships had returned . By 2.30 the British working feverishly had got back only 4 of the remaining ships . By the end of the afternoon the German High Seas Fleet , built at a cost of sixty milli pounds to rival England' lay at the bottom of Scapa Flow.

In I924 a London scrap metal firm began to salvage the German vessels . By I926 all of the destroyers had been raised . Year by year the bigger ships have been brought up and by I939 only 8 of the great ships remained at the bottom.

Scrap from the German fleet went into the Queen Mary and her sister ship the Queen Elizabeth . Much has also gone into Britain's armament programme and before the Home demand became too great some metal was even shipped to Germany .

Boat"
istmas

Issue No 32

Roll Call 0900 and 1600 Tuesday 7ᵗʰ March 1944

Toc H

There will be a meeting Toc-H in the Green Hut at ..m. on Wednesday . Visit are welcome .

The French Society will t in future from 8 to 9 . every Saturday .

Menu

ll Camp....Raisins &
         Barley.

---

ll Camp....I/5 th. tin
     Boiled beef, or
     Roast beef , or
     Sausage & tomato, or
     Lamb & Tomato
     Or...
     I/4 tin Tongue

Cook-house

Issue for the next two weeks will consist of I/2 Canadian parcel and I/2 ration of bulk per week per man .

New Zealand parcels issued this week were of three types , (I) With I chocolate and I pkt. raisins. (2) With two pkts. of raisins and (3) with I large veg, and no sugar .

Wanted

Wanted , pair of new shoes , size IO for new civilian boots , size IO

HOBSBAWN C7.

Red Cross Clothing

Will people who ordered boots and uniforms last month and who have not yet collect-ed them please do so before 7.p.m. tonight from the Clothing Office .

Barrack Shelves

It is believed that shelves will shortly be put along both walls in each room.

Will anyone knowing any-thing about Sgt.G.M.D. Bar-clay P.O.W. no.22645 ,LuftIII and Stalag 4B , please see Sgt. Stephenson D2.

THERE IS NO SICK PARADE THIS MORNING+

The "D.R." Ready Reckoner

We have had many requests for information regarding Income Tax and the ollowing is a scale made out by our Statistician:-

is.

	Single.		Married.		One Child.		Two Children	
	Income Tax.	Put to P. War Cred.	Income Tax.	Put to P War Cred.	Income Tax.	Put to P War Cred.	Income Tax.	Put to P War Cred.
	£ s d	£ s d	£ s d	£ s d	£ s d	£ s d	£ s d	£ s d
lots,) s. and) As.)	47.6.0.	13.17.0.	27.3.0.	7.17.0.	10.10.0.	3.0.0.	N.A.	N.A.
op.A/G	21.6.8.	6.4.0.	1.6.8.	0.8.0.	N.A.	N.A.	N.A.	N.A.
/G.	17.3.0.	4.6.0.	N.A.	N.A.	N.A.	N.A.	N.A.	N.A.
gineer	39.6.0.	11.12.0.	19.6.0.	5.12.0.	2.13.0.	0.15.0.	N.A.	N.A.
Sgts.								
lots,) s. and) As.)	64.0.0.	18.10.0.	40.13.0.	12.0.0.	24.0.0.	7.0.0.	7.13.0.	2.8.0.
op.A/G.	28.2.0.	8.3.0.	8.0.0.	2.6.0.	N.A.	N.A.	N.A.	N.A.
A/G.	22.13.4.	6.7.0.	2.12.0.	0.15.0.	N.A.	N.A.	N.A.	N.A.
os.								
lots,) s. and) As.)	78.0.0.	22.15.0.	49.6.0.	14.8.0.	32.13.0.	9.10.0.	16.0.0.	4.13.3.
op.A/G.	47.6.0.	13.7.0.	22.5.0.	6.5.0.	10.10.0.	3.0.0.	N.A.	N.A.
A/G.	39.10.0.	11.14.0.	27.3.0.	7.17.0.	5.0.0.	1.9.0.	N.A.	N.A.

Printed and Published by Macadam Press

A Peoples Government
It Depends on You

What has happened to the Beveridge Plan? At the moment it is most probably gathering dust in the archives of a Government Dept.

The adoption or rejection of the Beveridge Plan is a matter of national importance affecting almost every individual of the Nation , yet if this scheme of social security for all is once more placed centre stage in the spotlight of current affairs , the chances are that it will again become a bone of political contention to be chewed and worried and maybe finally tossed aside . If this is the case Mr. John Public will in all probability shrug his shoulders and go about his daily life as if the Beveridge Plan had never existed; or , if he does think about it , he will comfort himself with the thought " Well , what I say or do can have no effect in deciding such matters".

Far too often are such questions of nation wide import made the occasion for party squabbles , far too often do the Government panic the electorate into a disastrous course. What is the remedy ? The remedy lies with you . What is needed is common sense, logical action and application

Dont believe what your favourite newspaper tells you or your M.P. says or even what Bill Jones says at the Local. You know the facts , think about them and decide for yourself which course is the best . It does'nt need a detailed knowledge of economics or the machinery of Government--just common sense.

Once you have made up your mind , act . Write to your M.P. write to the appropriate govt.dept., you dont have to spend much time or energy in doing it.

" But ," says Mr.John Public, "I'm only one in 20 odd million , what good would my letter do ?"

This is a dangerously easy attitude to adopt , if nobody did anything nothing would ever be done . If everyone , or at least the majority, adopted the former course then public opinion would be really felt and it is a fact that no democratic government can withstand the weight of public opinion (remember the Hoare-Laval fiasco)

So when you return to Civvy street dont be a dog in the manger, dont, as is often the case, worry about your relatively minor affairs to the exclusion of questions of national importance which are in many cases settled by a comparitive handful of men without adequate refernece to the true state of public opinion.

It is'nt a question of politics--a government of a country is elected to carry out the wishes of the people--make that wish felt then perhaps we may get closer to government of the people by the people for the people '

140 Downed in Berlin Blit

The German radio reported yesterday that :

"On both sides Kriwoirog German troops again repulsed violent Soviet tacks or engaged them in the breached positions .

In the area of Swenigoodka and Schepatowka the heavy fighting continues undiminished in fury. A total of 41 tanks and 29 guns was destroyed south of Schepatowka.

On the main road Smole Orscha the Soviets continued in waves attempts at break through . The enemy in this sector lost 22 tanks .

In the far north mountain troops of the army and S.S. repulsed in the Louh sector several enemy atta with bloody losses to the enemy .

On the Italian front yesterday there was largely patrol and shock troop activity .

The attack of North America bomber formations against Berlin during the mid-day hours of yesterday brought large successes for the German air defences . The few residential areas in the area of Greater Berlin were hit by scattered bombs. 140 enemy aircraft of which 118 were 4-motored bombers were shot down .

Who's got a Red Neck

Last night Georgie Booth was asked how long he had been down . George friends told the enquirer who said to George " That all right , we're old Kriegies together -- I've been down two and a half years myself."

Note, Georgie is now well into his fifth year

...ewspaper Merger

...esterday the Editors of
"Daily Recco", after a
...ct conference, took over
...trol of the camp's Sun-
...paper , " The Compass"
This paper will keep its
...ginal name and will be
...ted by D.G.Adams and run
...m A3. The "Daily Recco"
...l continue, under the
...torship of A.Mackay and
...Whitlock , with offices
...89
...With these two papers ,
...hope to continue to give
... all the news as well
...topical and interesting
...icles on camp life .

Americans Settle Down

Americans in E Lager rep
ort that they are settling
down quickly and " Getting
on swell "with the other
nationalities in their compound . The difference in
slang still causes amuse-
ment .

They wish to make it kn-
own that they are also
pleased with the generosity
of their fellow prisoners.

160 new kriegies of
which 25 are British and
Dominions arrived yesterday

Queries

Did anyone definitely see
any engines on the large,
powered glider which flew
over the camp on Monday.

As there is a large bet
on this query, please bring
any gen to the Recco office.

We urgently require the
following shipping infor-
mation : What Line does the
S.S. Franconia belong to ?
What is her tonnage ?
Information to Recco office
please .

Volunteers are requested
to help on the football
pitch today . People prac-
ticing are asked to keep
off all parts of the pitch
which are being repaired .

Vhat are you going to say?

Rather an interesting
...int cropped up recently
...ring one of our Editor-
...l conferences. It was:
...at are you going to say
...out your P.O.W. life
...en you return to England?

This matter has been in
...e minds of most of us
...cently , especially af-
...r the news of the repat.
...ses arriving home.

On thinking it over ,
...consider this to be rath
...er a ticklish question.
...view of what appears to
...pear in P.O.W. Magazines
...e can hardly rush into
...e house and say " Moth-
..., I've been through
...ll..." It would fall
...ther flat , or else you
...most likely get the
...rse laugh.

On the other hand, no
...an worth his Red Cross
...rcel would go home and
...y that life in a P.O.W.
...amp had been wonderful,
...at the swimming pools
...d the beer gardens as
...blicised in the much
...oted P.O.W. Mags. were
...l that they had been
...acked up to be.

Then , no right think-
ing man likes to steer the
middle course and very few
of us are likely to be the
strong silent type that says
nothing. So , what shall
we tell 'em ?

Perhaps one of the best
ideas on this very ticklish
matter which we have heard
so far , is that of an imaginative Kriegie who
says.....
" I'll take 'em to a
film , and there are sure
to be many horror films por-
traying the matter , and ,
during the most horrific
part of the whole thing , I
shall dramatically whisper
....That was real....The
rest I shall leave to their
imagination .

We are inclined to agree
with this far thinking man
and say that much must be
left to the imagination .
Some of this life will make in
teresting and amusing stories after the war , some
must undoubtedly be left un-
told . Strong drink will
unquestionably bring out
some fine horror stories in
ex-Kriegies .It is a very
interesting subject for pit
dreaming . We leave it to
you .

TOC H

Toc-H meets tonight at
6 P.M. in the Green Hut

Red Cross

Two Wagons arrived last
night and will be unloaded
this morning .

The 47 sacks of personals
which arrived on Sat, will
be listed and issued as
soon as possible .

STOP   PRESS

Dai
"Freedom
293 [

M.B Splitters

"... I remember when we heard about your becoming a POW. I was at home at the time and I didn't feel well When I heard you were a POW I waxed and polished the floors and felt wonderful..

"... Darling, Please write more often as I do like the way you print..."

"... So you are in perfect health are you?..Wait till I get you home. You will know the meaning of bags under the eyes..."

"... And now to go from the sublime to the other extreme, your Mother came to see me yesterday..."

"... I took mother to the pictures the other night and a Canadian tried to get off with her..."

".... I broke a glass in the "Nag's Head" one night The Landlady asked me whether I would pay for it or put something in the Red Cross Box. I put 10/- in and she asked me if I would break another. I said I would if she did the same, but the old cat wouldn't play..."

From the ex-girl friend who married an Army Major and was asked to tell her Army friends, not too politely, to do something about the war:
"... I didn't understand your remark about the Army - but I don't suppose that you've heard the news lately or I'm sure you'd have said something quite different.."

"...You will pleased to hear that plans for de-mobilisation are being considered..."

Prison Camp Nerves

The following is an extract from a book dealing with conditions in a Turkish Prison Camp during last war.

"But every now and then a man would seek relief. As unostentatiously as might be he would change his Mess. He knew and we knew that he was not getting rid of the bonds that were so irksome. He was merely seeking to exchange the old for the new pattern of hand cuff in the hope that it would not gall him in the same raw spot. We could sympathize with him.

Your neighbour may be the most excellent of good fellows but if he is jogging your elbow for every hour of the twenty-four, you will begin to look askance at him Little idiosyncrasies that would pass unmarked in ordinary life assume the magnitude of positive faults.

The fine qualities of the man - his interests, his courage, his cheerfulness, his generosity - are lost to sight under the cloud of minor peculiarities that close acquaintance brings to view. His stoicism becomes a pose, his cheerfulness tomfoolery, his generosity softness and his courage rashness.

We knew the worth of the man beside us but we were being forced to examine them under a microscope.

"Z" was a glorious leader of men - we forgot it because he snored in his sleep."

Knowing that conditions here are similar and in the belief that the following will be of assistance to you, we publish an article from "The Readers' Digest".

"You probably think it

nothing unusual if you "Blow up", go to pieces, otherwise lose control of your emotions, yet the effect of these "Mental Sprees" on the health are almost as bad as the result of an alcoholic spree. People who indulge in "Mental Sprees" are sick - mentally sick, nervously disordered. They are victims of deficient self-control.

The trouble with most nervous people is that they are self-centred and introspective. They are wonderfully helped by anything that makes them get their minds on themselves.

No matter where the blame rests, if you allow other people to get on your nerves you are allowing their habits to tyrranize over you. You cannot control the habits of the rest of the world, therefore you must in self-protection learn to react with less vehemence. You must continue to live in this world as it

Query Answered

The S.S. Franconia is a Cunard-White Star Line vessel of 20,000 tons. She was built in the Cunard building programme soon after the last war as a transAtlantic Liner. She and sister ship the Laconia were used on the N.Atlantic crossing and were comfortable but slow. She was later commissioned as a "Floating Pub" for world cruises.

New Prisoners to go under Canvas
"Tents on Sportsfield" answer to Sports Space Plea

At the Conference with the Commandant held yesterday in the Vorlager, main business under discussion was points to be raised at the Protecting Power Meeting on Friday.

IN A SHORT TIME THE STRENGTH OF THE EXISTING THREE COMPOUNDS MAY BE BROUGHT UP TO 9,000 PRISONERS+

This Bombshell hit Sgt. Deans, Sgt. Mogg and the Leaders of 2 and 3 compounds when at the Conference Sgt. Deans requested more room for Sports Fields.

The Commandant stated that the extra men would have to be accomodated wherever possible. Five tents, each tent capable of holding 500 men would be provided.

The Commandant added that all recreational space would have to be used for the erection of tents to accomodate new prisoners.

This matter is to be brought up before the Protecting Power on Friday.

Red Cross

The two wagons which were unloaded yesterday contained 4200 rations of Bulk Food and 95 communal cigarette parcels.

The 47 sacks of personal parcels were listed yesterday. The clothing and cigarette parcels will be issued to-day.

Caledonian Society

At the General Meeting be held in the Green to-night at 7.30pm. k Isherwood will give alk on Life in the Bush. rs open at 7.20pm.

Cookhouse

For the next fortnight issue will be one Canan parcel and one week's ion of Bulk per man. The parcels will be issd on Monday of each k and the Bulk on Tuesand Wednesday March 14 15.
he Bulk issue is as folls:
ter...... 2/5 tin per m.
oolate.... 3/4 bar per m.
pping..... 1/4 per man.
ey or
.... 2/3 tin per m.
cuits... 1 1/7 per man.
k Jam..... 1/4 tin per m.

ARGENTINE MEATS
sh Stew..... 500 tins.
ned Beef.... 510 tins.
sages....... 510 tins.
ned Pork,... 510 tins.
out......... 500 tins.
w........... 1500 tins.

MENU
Camp - Sardines.

Camp - Corned Beef,
       Potatoes and
       Swede.

Mail

Three boxes containing 5 letters arrived yesday. All the letters e been distributed. re are now NO boxes out nding.

Britain, following the d of the U.S.A., has ken off Diplomatic Relons with the Argentine. (German Radio Report).

German Press News

Mr. Morrison, speaking on the Invasion said, "We will enter Europe, seize the German Army by the throat and shake it to Death. We intend to clear out the German General Staff and Military Tradition once and for all."
Later on he gave the losses of the English Army as:
73477 men killed and 152204 missing or POW. (These numbers do not include the Dominion casualties).

First Night

The All-Canadian Show - "Front Page" is opening in K Lager to-night.

Teething Trouble

Band Leader McNamara's K Lager Band Show was postponed owing to his Trombone player not having teeth. The trombonist's teeth were not forthcoming from the Dental Repair Shop in time for the Show.

WANTED
Pair of Gym. shoes size 6 or 7 for chocolate or cigarettes.
FOTHERINGHAM A 11.

M.B. Splitters

"... I hope you managed to have quite a decent time at Christmas. We didn't have too bad a time. Quite enjoyable, even if a little quieter than usual. On Boxing Day I went to an Engagement Party which lasted until seven o'clock next morning. You can guess I felt tired for a couple of days after..."

"...I'm sorry if there are long lapses between my letters to you. But I really don't seem to have much time to spare at nights. Tim came home for Xmas, went back a day later than he should have done and got seven days C.B. I know I'm nasty but I thought it funny. I'm still going strong with my American..."

From a house in which an R.A.F. Officer lives:
"... Nobody here knows anything about the Caterpillar Club..."

"... The fish-pond needs cleaning out but I don't think we'll have time for that..."

"... It has been announced that the Henry 8th. Chapel at Westminster Abbey is to become "Battle of Britain Chapel" as a National Memorial to those who fell..."

"...The paper this week has been telling us about the single-seat "sky runabouts" which Miles Aircraft are to produce after the war. They will cost about 150 and will be capable of management after 10 hours instruction. The family models will hold 3 or 4 and will cost 300 to 400. Every town will have a "runabout airfield."

Is it a Complex?

It appears that each of us has a dormant desire to "carve wood". At home with so many other interests at hand this craving is not felt so much.

We have noticed however, the number of men new to prison life - ourselves included - who sometimes, even before they had become acclimatised, start "whittlin'". The general tendency is for the new prisoners to make a model of whatever type of a/c in which they had flown. If by some rare chance the new Kriegie manages to complete this first effort then he may go on to making more models of different a/c types.

In the still more unlikely event of the prisoner, after say two years, having exhausted the a/c types he will then cast his talents into the Clock-making Business - a thriving trade in this compound.

In this case his tablemates will be eating tin-filings along with whatever meal the Cook-house turns out. It may noticed at this point that more hardened Kriegies than "that" have been driven into other rooms as a result of having a tame Clock-maker around.

This clock-making phase we are glad to say does not last very long.

After this the prisoner having one thing in common with us - a desire for the war to end, eventually becomes so weary waiting for The Boat that he starts model ship-building.

The clock-making and boat-building stages of the prisoner's development show his subconcious attitude to the passage of time and the ever-present longing for his return home.

Editorial

Following the example set by the Daily Recco at Sagan and again here, there has recently come in to force a spate of news-sheets. This is in the main a good scheme for providing members with interesting local news.

At the same time we take a very poor view of those papers which include in their Mail columns news is not of purely local interest. By bringing the general news items to us the greatest number in the compound - in all three compounds - benefits.

We have seen in two of these district papers Mail Bag Gen which would have interested and amused you the Public. We have also heard that other Clubs will in future publish Mail gen. This M.B. Splitter column in the Daily Recco is run for everyone's benefit. It is up to you to see that YOU benefit by it.

MAIL
It is believed that there may be some mail at the Heydekrug express office.

Recce

Boat
stmas

ter-Compound ccer Team r Sunday

ootball President Bryce
unced yesterday that in
event of the ground be-
too hard for the inter-
ound Rugby game on Sun
E Lager will bring a
over to play Arsenal.
reason for picking Ars
to play was that there
three teams with no pla
in the Inter-compound
: two of these teams
already played this
on. Arsenal is the
d.
Referee for the A-K
is Hill K Lager.
.ger's team is:-
th: Simpson, Davies:
ener, Payne, Blackburn:
, Hibbs, Ross, Martyn,
Harris.

p P.o.W. Mail

From a letter comes the
s that the first card
a prisoner in Japanese
nds who was captured at
gapore, has been receiv
by his parents.
The card was in the form
a Field Postcard, type-
tten and 25 words long.
soners are allowed to re
ive only two letters 25
is long per month.

Education

Anyone wishing to take
uary Matriculation parts
r 2 are asked to hand to
ir names in to the Ed-
tion Office by Saturday
h. March.
Probable date for the
mination is April 3rd.

AVE MILK NOW. SAVE MILK NOW . SAVE MILK NOW.

Cook-house
Another Spud Ration Cut

The potato ration has
been cut to 400 grams. Careful peeling is now essen-
tial.

The Argentine Bulk Issue
meats for the next fortnigh
have been so arranged that
the whole camp will get the
same amounts of each partic
lar item .i.e. Instead of
two blocks having lamb and
two blocks having steak and
onions, the whole camp will
get either one or the other
This has been made poss-
ibly by the co-operation of
E & K Lagers .

YOU ARE AGAIN REMINDED TO
SAVE YOUR MILK . There may
be two consecutive fort-
nights of bulk .

M E N U
All Camp.. Corned Meat,
    German meat extra.
B 7 8 & 9 German beef
    steaks and roast pot-
    atoes.
All Camp... 1/5 tin of
    Boiled beef or 1/4 tin of
    tongue.

Football Practice

The Compound football
team is having a kick around
this morning at 10.30.
People are requested to
keep clear of the West Goal

Red Cross

46 sacks of personals
arrived late yesterday .
They will be sorted and list
ed as soon as possible .

Vacancy

There are two vacancies
in the spud room staff .
Anyone wanting these jobs,
please see Sgt. Brown i/c
spud room .

Wanted

Wanted , one china mug
for cigarettes.
    MURRAY B9

Wanted , American leather
type jacket in exchange for
a 20 inch by 25 inch portrait of the owner. No exchange
unless model is completely
satisfied with the portrait.
    COLES AI

German Radio

Forces of American bombers
and fighters suffered heavy
losses in their mid-day
attack on Berlin on Wednesday.
German air defence forces
shot down 112 enemy aircraft
66 of which were 4-motored
bombers . A few districts
of the city suffered damage
and the population had small
losses.
The Japanese have launch-
ed a general offensive against
the Torokina beachhead on the
island of Bougainville with
heavy reinforcements. Two
airfields have been stormed
and captured.
Near Kertsch several
enemy attacks were repulsed
in the breakthrough area
S.W. of Kriwoirog. In the
area of Swenigorodka and S.W.
of Jampol the German troops
offered stubborn resistance
to the advancing enemy. On
one sector 52 enemy tanks were
destroyed . On the main
Smolensk-Orscha road the
Soviets continued their violent breakthrough attacks
without success . All attacks
collapsed in the defensive
fire of all types of weapons
from the German lines .
In the far north the So-
viets launched attacks with
superior forces , but were
repulsed . A Soviet landing
attempt on the Fisherman's
peninsula. was also frustrated.
In Italy there was only
local shock troop activity.

68

109

M.B. Splitters

"...It would be no surprise to us to learn that you had been having another removal as that area should soon be resounding to the tramp of retreating marching feet - or probably it would be nearer the truth to say the "hasty tramp" for that is what it amounts to..."

"... Please let me know the thing you fancy most when you return..."
(From a Mother).

"... I see by the paper yesterday that an Aussie flyer fell 1500 feet without his chute opening, when he hit the ground he went on for another three feet. When they dug him out they found that he had broken every bone in his body. He is now ready to resume operations again..."

"...To-night's papers tell of an American tail-gunner who fell from his 'plane without his chute. He fell 100 feet, rolled 100 yards and only received a sprained ankle minor cuts and bruises lucky Devil..."

"... Two pounds of grapes cost 2. 5/-..."

"... The Bombing of Essen was on show at the Glasgow Art Galleries on January 6th..."

"... Mrs. Taylor, the insurance man's Wife from across the road, has given you half a pound of chocolate.. Her brother was repatriated and said he did not need it..."

Barth in Action Zone
New Arrivals see Blitzed Towns

The seven men who came into the Camp from Barth yesterday morning brought the following news:

The Camp Leader is Wing Commander Hilton. Stren is now about 2000 increasing weekly. There are fou Lagers.

The newcomers report that there are about three Raid Alarms daily. Aircraft are rarely seen but th noise of machine-guns and cannons is heard. A .5 m ine gun bullet link was picked up in the Camp. On night raid on Berlin, it took British Bombers three quarters of an hour to pass over the Camp.

On their way to this Camp they passed through hea ily damaged towns. At Stettin the factory area and railway station are blitzed: at Anklem the large a/ works is badly damaged and at Marienberg there is a severe damage and the bridge over the river is demol ished.

The seven men confirmed the report of a new R.A. Camp at Marienberg and they stopped for a night at Canadian Camp at Stargard. This Camp which is very well built has concrete roads: the prisoners are Die Boys.

At Barth there has been a recent outbreak of Menin gitis with one fatality - Lieutenant Thomas. The Camp is also reported to be infested with Crabs.

Returned Sick See German Killed

The party of seven men who left this Camp on March 7th, to go to Stablach for special treatment returned yesterday without receiving complete treatment.

It appears that on the w way to the Hospital the train in which they were travelling hit a German civ ilian sitting on a cart of logs which was crossing the line. The cart overturned and the civilian was thrown into a flooded ditch. The logs rolled on top of him, pinning him down in the ditch where he drowned.

CONTD. FROM PREVIOUS CO

On the journey back t party travelled in the s train as the relatives o the dead man who were go t his funeral.

This party which arri at the hospital at 10 am were inspected by the Fr doctors and told for how long they would be kept. At 1.30pm. they were ord ed to leave by the Germa Authorities who told the that the hospital was fo French patients only and not for British and Amer ican casualties.

Special Wanted

Sgt. Coles A 1, wants an American Leather Jacke in exchange for a 20"x25" portrait of its owner in oils. No payment unless sitter is satisfied.

...oat
...ristmas..

Roll Calls 0900 and 1600 Saturday 11ᵗʰ March 1944

...ore food in Bulk ...an in B.R.C.

...Two wagons left Geneva ...March 3rd., containing ...k Food equivalent to ...25 .rations.

...To clarify the position ...arding Bulk Issue, it ...decided to make a list ...the comparative weights ...the various issues made ...the Compounds. ...Consequently the weight, ...luding packing, was ...nd and the following re- ...s obtained:

...ish Red Cross - ...355 Kilos. per man. ...adian Red Cross - ...245 Kilos. per man. ...k Issue - ...752 Kilos. per man.

...It was also suggested ...the meat content was ...below that of the par- ...s. The weight was then ...n of the meats in each ...e and the results are: ...ish Red Cross - ...65 Kilos. per man. ...adian Red Cross - ...55 Kilos. per man. ...k Issue - ...94 Kilos. per man.

...t should be noted how- ...that the meat content ...oth British Red Cross ...Bulk Issue does not in- ...e, in the case of B.R.C. ...tables or Soup Powders. ...Vegetables in the case ...he Bulk Issue.

Record Recital

...he weekly Gramophone ...tal will be held in the ...tre at 13.30 hours to- ...ow, Sunday March 12th. ...are asked to note the ...red time. Programme is ...n on the Notice Board.

Cook-house

The New Zealand parcels which did not contain sugar had instead a tin of Meat and Vegetables which was put in the Communal Store.

As there were very few of these parcels the sugar will be replaced.

Note: This only applies to New Zealand parcels.

M E N U
Saturday:
All Camp - Cold Salmon and Potatoes.
C4 -611 - Fishcakes.

All Camp - Corned Meat, Swede & Potatoes

Sunday:
All Camp - Canadian Bully Hash & Swede.

All Camp - N.Z. Hot Pot and Potatoes.

No Mail In

Will claimants for the following letter please call at the Camp Office.
To: My Dear Bill,
From: Sister Jean,
Address: Apt. 26
21 Avenue Road,
Toronto 5.
Ontario.
There is NO mail at the station.

Return Skates

You are requested to re- turn all Communal Skates to the Sports Store at once.

Query

Our latest query is the cause for a great deal of argument in a certain room. If you can answer it call in at the Recco Office: "Has Gt. Britain ever re- ceived coal from Italy?

Chess Problem ... No 4

B B							
		W Q					
				W K			
				W P			
						B P
					B K	W Kt

White to play and mate in 4

Wanted

Wanted Polo-neck sweater in exchange for any other item of clothing and/or very generous offer of cig- arettes (up to 1000).
GULPAN   A 1.

Uman Evacuated

The German Radio reported yesterday that:
" At noon North American Bomber formations carried out anothe Terror attack on Berlin. H.E. and incendiaries were dropped through thick cloud on various parts of the city and suburbs causing damage and high civilian losses.

Districts in W. and N. Ger- many were also raided, but the German Air Defences only shot down 9 a/c.

The town of Uman was evacuated During the heavy fighting in this area 91 Russian tanks were destroyed.

West of Kirowograd, S.W. of Swenigorodka, S. of Schep- etowka and S.W. of Jampol great battles are continuing with ever increasing fury. On some sectors the Soviet attacks were held but on others the Russians succeded in thrusting further forward.

Published by
Mackay-Whitlock Press

Dail
"Freedor
288 I

MB Splitters

"... Darling, dont keep saying you look 45. Anyhow I'll soon make you feel youthful again..."

"... Our POW Fund is quite a flourishing affair. If you would like some cigarettes would you write and ask Col. Elliott (he's the big noise) for a package to be sent..."

"... I've just been reading in the paper(so it is no secret now) that we are making jet-propelled planes they fly at a tremendous speed without a propellor. The inventor is G/C. Frank Whittle. The paper also tells us that the Germans are producing hundreds of little Pilotless Bombers to bomb us. They say they can be catapulted from the ground and steered by radio..."

"... You remember ------- who married a Pole? Well she has just had a baby boy. She said to her Polish husband that she would like the baby to be called Sandy Her husband said that he didn't care if it was called Sandy, Monday or Tuesday..."

From a sister being married on January 5th. Letter written in December:
"... Well I shall be getting married soon however I don't expect you will manage to be back in time.."

The following is written by one of the 8th. Army Boys in Italy to his mother
"... Get a good crease in my flannels..."

"... We had a Utility Turkey at Christmas - a sausage with a feather in it..."

Protecting Powe Visit

Attache' Msr. W. Braun and secretary Ms Wagner, representatives of the Protecting Power vis the Camp on Friday March 10th. A conference was he with Sgts. Deans, Mogg, Lunsford and Clarke.

The attaché was told that Polish and Czech POWs had arrived recently at the Camp.

The attache referred to the stripping of N.C.Os. during Gestapo searches: he stated that the Commandant could not be held responsible as the Special Police were enpowered to carry out periodic searches of prisoners Such searches must be carrie out in a decent manner - the P.P. to be informed if this were not done and they would do all possible to see that searches were carried out in accordance with the Geneva Convention.

The attache promised to take up the matter of the lack of accomodation in the Sick Bay with the Commandan and High Command. The Drs. informed the attache of the shortage of dressings and asked for two more Doctors and a Dental Officer. The attache had no knowledge of the coming of the next Medical Commission but promise to enquire.

Msr. Braun promised to press for action in the matter of the transfer of Dominion and Colonial prisoner to warmer climates.

Sgt. Deans requested a scale of treatment for NCOs in Arrest and the attache said that he would try to secure it.

The point regarding Cour Martial for damage to German property was discussed: the attache said that men would not be liable to Courts Martial for such trivial acts as cutting the wire in at-

tempt to escape - on the other hand if prisoners took Reich property with them on escapes they wou then be liable to such a charge.

Msr. Braun promised enquire into the Censor at Sagan, to speed up m delivery and to look int the matter of facilities for Telegrams to Next-o Kin.

He said that he ask an R.C. Padre to be sen here as soon as possible eneral shortage of ing equipment was broug up. It was stated that the position would be ba when the Camp increased 9000. Mr. Braun promise to take the matter up ar commented that he was gl to see the Communal cook ing of Red Cross Food in this camp as it was by the most economical and ficient way of dealing it. Sgt. Deans said tha it might be so if cookin facilities were adequate The attache also promise to look into the matter fresh vegetables.

After a request that shutters, on both sides the hut should be permit to be left open after lights out the attache s he would talk with the Commandant.

There was considerab discussion about the supply and storage of R Cross Food Reserves. Deans said that the pre

NTD. FROM PREVIOUS COL.

...rage facilities were in-
...quate and would be even
...se with an increase to
...O men when a reserve of
...000 parcels would be re-
...red. At present camp
...ength the reserve was
...y of 7 weeks duration
... the number of prisoners
... increasing daily. Mr.
...un said that he would
... the R.C. as soon as
...ssible. Sgt. Deans said
...had already telegraphed
...m.

The attache sauid he wou
...ld look into the matter
... lack of clothing repair
...ilities.

He promised to try to
...ain for the prisoners a
...y of the Official scale
...rations issued by the
...man Authorities.

Sgt. Deans complained o
... lack of recreation
...ce which was bad already
... when the Sportsfields
...e used for tents the
...ditions would be even
...rse. Mr. Braun stated
...t he and the Commandant
...e of the same opinion
...Sgt. Deans: he promised
...report the matter and
...so the matter of over-
...owding in barracks. Sgt.
...ns suggested that organ-
...ed walks should be per-
...tted - these were essenti
... to the health of the
...up if sports facilities
...e not possible.

M E N U

1 Camp - Sultanas and
          Barley.
----
1 Camp - Canadian Meat
          Roll, Peas and
          Potatoes.

If anyone has the copy
... the Lonsdale Book of
...xing will they please
...urn it to G. BOOTH B 5.

Eisenhower Gives Pep Talk

Yesterday's German Radio
reported that:

"General Montgomery in a
speech to armament workers
said, "The second front has
already begun, and the invasion of the Continent will
be a simple thing,"

General Eisenhower at a
Troop Centre said, " Auf-
Wiedersehen - East of the
Rhine".

Before mid-day yesterday
American Bomber Forces carried out a blitz on the Mun-
ster area. Damage was small
Last night a few nuisance
raiders bombed W. Germany.
3 a/c were shot down by
Flak.

In Italy American bombers
attacked Padua and Florence
In violent air battles and
by Flak 30 enemy a/c were
shot down, 11 of them by
National Italian Fighters.
Toulon was also raided.

Communal Cig. Fund

The raffle in aid of the
Communal Cigarette Fund
will take place within the
next few days.

E Lager has sent letters
of thanks over for contributions made to them. Below
we publish a few extracts:
"Thanks very much for the
cigarettes...They will be
distributed as sparingly as
possible... The new arrivals
here think it's a very good
show".

In recognition of the
discipline the Commandant
has seen on visits to the
camp, he has decided to can
cel Sunday afternoon roll-
calls. This will continue
as long as our discipline.
continues.

Competition

Winners of last week's
Mail Gen competition are
Sgt. Dance C 10 and the person in K Lager who submitted
the item about going to stud

Cigarettes this week go
to the person guesses cor-
rectly the number of ReccO
readers between 10 and 11am.
for the week. Pencil and
paper alongside.

Dental Repair

Will the person who hand-
ed in the partial repair
denture to the Dental Repair
Shop please see Chas. Dare
A 8. The denture had four
teeth on it and one missing.

Yesterday's Shooting

Yesterday morning a pris-
oner jumped over the warning
wire to retrieve a ball.
The guard in the North box
fired and the shot missed
the offender by ten yards.
The bullet hit the ground
a few inches from an innocent
bystander and spattered him
with earth.

The consequences of this
incident might have been far
more serious.

You are again requested
NOT to go over the warning
wire on any condition.

Wanted

Wanted stiff-back quarto
or f'scap exercise book for
attractive offer of cigarettes
SHAW A 7.

More Air-Raid Damage

A burnt-out personal par-
cel has been received in the
compound. The parcel which
was repacked at Potsdam,
contained only burnt chocolate and the remains of a
shirt and towel. A bill was
attached for the cost of re-
packing - four marks.

M.B. Splitters

"... I had a letter from my brother in which he accused me of becoming an old maid. Was I mad? I wrote to him right away and told him that though I might appear to be old according to his infantile outlook, I am certainly not the other thing..."

"... When next I see your pal, I will ask him to get tickets for you and I for the coming Cup Final..."

"... The bus is just around the corner, we have turned the corner, the bus is in sight, you will be in time and there is plenty of room for all..."

"... I am an Aylesbury fellow, repatriated from Germany, and I am a straightforward fellow, so I must do my duty by letting you know that I am going to marry your girl. If there is anything you want us to do for you we will be only too pleased to do it. I hope you will not take it too bad..."

"... Mr. Wimpy the dog, has taken it into his head that it is too far to walk back here each evening after an all-day scrounge around the Town. So he comes home by bus. We have heard quite a lot about his travelling on the bus but at last he has been rumbled. You are supposed to pay farebfor a dog and it appears the the conductresses have asked in the bus who owns the dog. Yesterday the same thing happened when it was founddout that no-one owned him, he was put off at a stop down the road. However to-day he arrived in at the bus time on another free ride..."

German Radio

Yesterday's German radio reported that:

"British Bomber and Torpedo aircraft on the twelfth of March attacked the German steamer CIUSSI in Spanish territorial waters off the mouth of the Ebro. They set the ship on fire and it was sunk.

The focal point of the great Soviet attacks is unchanged on the southern sector of the East Front. German troops put up stubborn resistance to the superior attacking Russian forces. In the heavy fighting yesterday they repulsed many attacks.

In the breakthrough area S.W. of Kirwoirog, S.W. of Uman and East of Tarnopol, the Soviet spearheads were held up after the destruction of a large number of tanks.

Is this your Card?

The following postcards are lying in the Camp Office without the Absender details filled in:
Mrs. G. Peacock, Manitoba.
Signed........ Clem.
L.A.C. J.W.Lobb, Can. Base Post Office, England.
Signed.........Bernard.
Miss Joan Rawson, Leeds.
Signed.........Bob.
Miss Peggy Mitchell, Haigh, near Barnsley, Yorks.
Signed........ Bob.
Mr. and Mrs. Jackson, Old Coulsdon, Surrey.
Signed........ ?
Mrs. Mackenzie, La Tour de Peilz, Suisse.
Signed........ F.C.
Miss E.M. Moore, Southall, Middx.
Signed.........Alan.
Miss M. Butcher, Bitterley, Shropshire.
Signed.........Den.

The Car o[f]

OUTSTANDINGLY [...] car of the future - a fut[...] as time goes.

It will be an automobi[le] carrying its engine in th[e] rear: this placement of t[he] power plant will make for [...] far greater motoring comf[ort] and greater roominess.

The body of the car of [...] the future, even to its w[ind]shield and windows, will [...] of new synthetic material [...] probably some forms of m[ould]ed plastics. In this car [...] will be found the last w[ord] in devices that will make [...] for the safety of driver [...] and passengers - windows [...] and windshields of clear [...] transparent substances, w[hich] neither shatter nor fly u[n]der impact and thus do n[ot] cut: airplane type "crash [...] pads" to protect occupant[s] from hard bumps in road a[c]cidents.

While every car drive[r] is greatly intrigued by [...] sweeping inovations in m[...] or car designs he has not [...] the ability nor the inher[...]ent willingness to accept [...] great changes rapidly.

Suppose the manufacture[r] suddenly "transplanted" [...] motor from the front to [the] rear of the car - the dr[iver] would feel exposed to all [...] sorts of dangers. So the [...] of the future, even thou[gh] its engine is in the rea[r] must be designed to have [...] the semblance of a hood.

The power plant will [...] up far less space in the [...] tail of the car than the [...] gine does now. The trend [...] wards elimination of run[...]ning boards is making po[s]sible far wider bodies. [...] rear end placement of th[e] engine and utilisation o[f] former running board spa[ce] can offer from 25 to 35% [...]

114

he Future

erent will be the motor hat is not far distant,

re interior space.

In view of the strides h the development of plas c material in the last w years, it is reasonabl believe that future cars ll be of plastic material cause colour is an in - erent part of plastics, ere will be no nedd for inting the new type auto obile and no danger of ding and chipping.

Use of transparent plas cs will make possible rved airplane type win- ws and windshields, whose ntours can be made to "low in" with the lines o he car. Such synthetic ass is available to-day d, clear as real glass, ll admit healthful ultra olet rays and exclude in- a-red rays of sunlight. al glass does not do this

By means of complete r conditioning the driver ll be able to create whatever type of "weather" e desires by simply setti handy control dial. A hermostatic element will the rest. The car will t need windows of the onventional type with evers and handles to ad- st them. The windows of lastic "glass" can be in- talled permanently. Thus here will be no draughts.

The car of the future, y virtue of its greater oominess and comfort can e literally made a lux- rious "home on wheels".

One wagon containing 00 rations of Bulk Food d 50 boxes of cigarettes s unloaded yesterday.

Something in your Line

"Farm hand - no work to do - must be able to sit in Rocking Chair in cool South Porch and come to meals un- assisted. wages $75 per month, room and board. En- quire in person after15.00 hours on 16th.-17th. Dixon Cherry County, M.O."

What a job for an ex- Kriegie, but in actual fact five men tried to stick this job out and the longest quitted after three weeks. Complaints were that it was "too hot".

ANY TAKERS?

Technical Library

Will all people having Building and Architectural Books from the Technical Library, whether they be on permanent or weekly loan, please return them on Tues- day March 14th., for check- ing prposes.

Look your 'Geographic Mags' Over

There are a number of Geographical Magazines at present going round the rooms. Would room leaders ask if anyone has the num- ber in which there is an article on Berlin, please bring it to the Camp Office

Land D S Debate

The Commandant has per- mitted 100 men from Lager 3 to visit Lager 1 from 1.30 to 3.30pm. on Wednesday 15th March to take part in the inter-compound Debate.

Chess Solution

Key Move:
1. Q-Q2, Black moves.
2. K-B4, "   "
3. K-Kt.3, "   "
4. Q MATES on KB2, KKt.2, or KR2.

Wanted

Wanted 2 pairs of summer nderpants in exchange for Van Heusen type shirt, col- lar attached, size 15.
FORMAN C 2.

Wanted 5000 cigarettes in exchange for scale model 15 foot, half-deck sailing dinghy clinker-built, 60 cms. long.
HOLLIDGE A 11.

Wanted Norwegian Grammar in exchange for cigarettes.
OLSEN D 5.

Wanted Elementary Spanish Grammar in exchange for Ger- man Elementary Grammar.
BARRY A 5.

+++ HARRY'S +
+   BUSTER+++
+

See Notices for details.

Teaspoon Lost

Will the person who was lent a teaspoon by Sgt. Green algh on Friday please re- turn it. It is believed that the borrower is in E Lager.

Caledonian Society

The dancing class will be held to-night at 5.15pm. in the Green Hut, instead of on Friday as previously advert- ised.

Query

How many sides to the new hreepenny pieces? Answers to the ReccO Office.

STOP PRESS

Dail
"Freedor
28b Dc

M.B. Split

Two gentlemen in the compound recently formed a private company - Sparrow Catchers, Ltd. About 30 sparrows in all were caught, most of them set free carrying messages to England, but some of them were eaten. Here a snag arose and the company dissolved because the junior partner after plucking and roasting the birds on a spit, woofed both his and his partner's share.

The method used was the old English Brick-trap, whereby the incautious sparrow, which alights to take the bread-bait, is beaned by half a house-brick and popped smartly into the box.

The experts state that the winter is the best period of the year to set traps. The snow is on the ground and there is little natural bird food. Furthermore, it is essential that an operation to be successful, is not hindered by onlookers.

We understand that roast sparrow tastes very much like a smaller edition of roast partridge.

In Germany all birds are protected by law - therefor all operations must be secret.

If anyone thinks that this is all so much hogwash, the gentlemen in question will produce a live sparrow for any bet up to 500 cigarettes.

Barron Harvest

Sgt. Barron, who has contributed many cigarettes for Missing advts., has at last found his slide rule.

During B 7's session of Pitopoly it was discovered underneath his bed.

Music-lover's Ple
Amplifier Draws Crowds to Recito

Not one of the little band of enthusiasts the first Sunday afternoon Music Recital given in this Camp would have been prepa to forecast that within nine months a programme of more difficult works of Brahms and Wagner would attr an audience too large for the Theatre to accomodate. But amazing as it is, this has actually occurred.

The history of these recitals has been one long story od inceeased attendances, and although the promoters of Sunday's Concert must have doubted the popularity of such works as Brahms' 1st. Symphony and Wagner's "Faust" Overture, music lovers in the Camp evidently did not, and the hall was overcrowded.

What is the reason for this popularity? Is it that Kriegies will attend anything to pass away an afternoon? We do not think so, otherwise the previous concerts given at Sagan would have been more successful.

No, the explanation is to be found in the fact that a large proportion of the men in this Camp are awakening to the appreciation of good music, and now that we have an amplifier, they realise that the works of the World's Great est Composers as interpreted by the World's most famous Artists can now be heard almost to Concert perfection.

There was great disappointment in many quarters when the "Serenade" and "Celebrity" Concerts were discontinued. They could always command a full house when the apparatus available was a pathetically inadequate gramophone. One

can well imagine the fig for admission that would ensue if it were possibl for these programmes to re-commenced with the ai of the amplifier.

We now possess a Libr of nearly a thousand records, ranging from Ligh Classical to the greates Symphony Music in existe Unlimited entertainmet stowed away in boxes. An hundreds of men clamouri to hear them.

Can the members of th Entertainments Committee shut their eyes to this new development in enter tainment? Surely the de sire of so many for more frequent recitals is wor of a few more hours per week in the Theatre programme. At least the su gestion is worthy of the most serious considerati of the Entertainments Co mittee whenever the ques ion of the allocation of Theatre Times comes up f consideration.

"The greatest good fo the greatest number", mu be the slogan.

Sick Parades

You are again reminde that if you wish to go s you must hand your name to the M.I. Room overnig between 6.00 and 7.00pm.

We emphatically point out that it is not suffi ent to attach to yoursel to the parade at the Mai Gate.

ReecD

"Boat"
...ristmas

Issue no 39

Roll Calls 0900 and 1600 Wednesday 15th March 1944

Book Censoring

The Book Censor has not ...e any work on books so ...this week. There are ...r 1000 personal and com...al books awaiting the ...sor's stamp.

...ill anyone who knows ...Sgt. George Stuart Brown ...adian POW., please call ...the Camp Office.

Joe Fulkerson Back

Bass-player Joe Fulkerson is back in the Sick Bay after a visit to Heydekrug to have his appendix removed.

Tea Issue At Last.

To-day there will be an issue of: 1/2 pkt. Canadian Tea per man: 1/2 pkt. Raisins and one pkt. Prunes.

Cherson Evacuated

Yesterday's German Radio reported that:

"In the course of the disengaging movement the town of Cherson was evacuated after the destruction of all war installations.

On the Southern sector of the East Front, in continued thaw conditions, the great struggle continues. Both sides are pouring in fresh reinforcements.

A German submarine chaser sank an enemy submarine in the Mediterranean.

6

Wanted

Wanted Senior Servoce cigarettes etc. for John Cotton's No.1 medium pipe tobacco.

ARNOTT A 10.

Wanted cigarettes for Irvin jacket.

SKAN   A 7.

Wanted wrist-watch for new pair civvy boots size 9 and cigarettes.

ADDERLEY   C 2.

Tickets for Debate

Tickets for the intercompound Debate will be issued at the Booking Office this morning between 10.00 and 11.00am. These tickets will be issued to people who have been paper-speakers or floor-speakers at past debates.

STOP PRESS

"I decided to open a second front" FROM Notziger

Postings

...0 men are expected to ...ive in this compound ...n E Lager to-day. ...t is believed that 180 ...arrivals are on the way ...majority of them being ...cans.

...e German Authorities ...granted permission for ...change of prisoners ...en this Lager and ...ager

MENU

All Camp - Salmon. Prunes.

All Camp - Sausages, beans and potatoes.

TOC H

The above society will meet in the Green Barrack at 6.00pm. to-night. Visitors are welcome. Bring your own stools.

3d

12 Sides.

Camp humour

The Turning of the Tide

While the increasing number of prisoners coming into the camp was creating problems for the Germans, they were also creating problems for the Kriegies themselves.

Accommodation was tight with many sacrifices having to be made – by men who felt they had sacrificed enough already. There were problems with Red Cross supplies and the older Kriegies knew just how vital these were to the daily job of keeping body and soul together. There was resentment – again among the older Kriegies – that circumstances had forced a change from the old independent way of prisoners getting their Red Cross parcels to themselves to do with as they would. Now communal cooking was the order of the day and, despite the recommendation of the protecting power that it was the most economical way of dealing with the food, many of us preferred our old independence. Added to that was the fact that the German rations, never of the best quality and seldom of sufficient quantity, had become even scarcer. It was a time of belting-up for everyone.

To overcome the difficulties – for themselves – some astute prisoners had adopted a line of action which forced us to issue a public warning in the issue of March 29, 1944:

SPUDS SMUGGLED FROM COOKHOUSE

During the last few days several people have been seen scrounging around the potato peeling dump.

This was allowed because it was believed that only small parts of potatoes were being collected.

On investigation, however it was found that certain rooms were leaving whole potatoes amongst the peelings with the intention of collecting them later. In fact, in one case several men were seen filching full Red Cross boxes of potatoes.

As a warning to those concerned, it is announced that the cookhouse staff know which rooms are indulging in this mean trick at the expense of their fellows.

If this state of affairs continues those rooms whose members are participating in this thieving racket, will have their potato ration severely cut.

Room leaders of all rooms, except A8 and D11, are asked to co-operate by seeing that no raw potatoes are cooked in their rooms.

The camp was split into the haves and have-nots. The former, because of length of service behind barbed wire had accumulated little private hoards of food, clothing and cigarettes, the result of careful hoarding of Red Cross or personal parcels over the years. The have-nots were those Kriegies who lived from day to day with no thought of the morrow, confident that something would turn up and they would be looked after or, more frequently, they were new prisoners who had not been in the can long enough to accumulate any of the worldly goods by which the Kriegies laid great store – usually cigarettes.

Bartering was a way of life in the German prison camps. We saw, in those dark days, the first multicoloured swap shop – Foodacco – where prisoners, flush in some commodity, would take it into the store for trading against something else, or simply to leave it in store against a rainy day – there were sure to be many. Private trades were done every day all over the camp, usually between members of the same combine or within the same barrack. And as the columns of the *Daily Recco* revealed, there was also a widespread trade done through our Wanted ads. The state of the economy – by which I mean the amount of food available – could be judged over the years by the switching of adverts from books, clothing, etc, in exchange for cigarettes, the common currency, to straight swaps for food.

On Thursday, April 6 we published an article warning that trading with the Americans in E Lager had to cease – to save the American prisoners from themselves. The Yanks came with leather bomber jackets and double-breasted shirts which proved an instant attraction with the old British Kriegies. Dependent on the cupidity of the old Kriegie, the avidity of the Yank for fags and, occasionally the current rate of exchange at the time, the prized articles of clothing were exchanged for anything from 50 to 500 cigarettes. Many of the Yank prisoners, while puffing away merrily on English cigarettes, sat shivering in their draughty barracks, wearing the absolute minimum of clothing. So it was on April 6 we published:

CAMP LEADERS VETO CLOTHING TRADING

Inter-compound trading has reached the point where it is harmful to the interests of prisoners in E Lager for it to continue.

This state of affairs has arisen owing to the trading of clothes for cigarettes. There is at present an acute shortage of clothing in E Lager. As we already know, the receiving and fitting out camp at Dulag has been destroyed together with its stock of clothing, so that new arrivals, particularly Americans, are forced to come here dressed only in flying kit and underclothes. The flying kit is confiscated by the German authorities.

The already low stocks of clothing in the camp store are not able to stand up to this extra strain on resources and each new prisoner is issued with the bare minimum of clothing.

Sgt Paules, E Lager compound leader, has realised this and together with Sgt. Deans and Sgt. Clarke of K Lager, has decided that it is in the best interests of the camp that all inter-compound trading must stop as the majority of new arrivals are Americans and the strain of helping them out will fall principally on the prisoners in E Lager.

All men in E Lager who have access to the *Vorlager* have been instructed to act in their official capacity only and not to carry on trading with other Lagers, either on their own behalf or for their friends.

It is a ruling in E Lager that cigarettes, etc, coming into the compound for trading purposes, will be confiscated and handed over to the Red Cross for distribution as they see fit.

It is also a ruling that any individuals in E Lager attempting to trade will have that clothing confiscated. It will be turned over to camp stores and issued to a new prisoner who needs it.

Just how serious the situation was developing in the spring of 1944 was brought home on April 16 when, after losing another issue through censorship, we published a warning to our fellow Kriegies to start hoarding. For as the fortunes of war turned in the favour of the Allies, bringing joy to our hearts, conditions for us and our German guards became steadily worse. The threat of a sudden move from the camp was ever present; the guards were bad-tempered and aggressive; the German stews and soups reached the stage when individual barley seeds could be counted in each bowlful handed out. It was the time for airmen to turn into squirrels.

PRECAUTIONS NECESSARY

We bring to your notice a remark made by the Camp Leader Sgt. Deans at the meeting of the Mess committee:

I can only advise people, he said, to save whatever they can out of the dry foods in their parcels.

Sgt. Deans is an old Kriegie and he knows what he is talking about.

Inadequacy of Reserve

Those who are new to prison life might, with some justification, point out that it is impossible to save anything like an adequate reserve against a complete stoppage of Red Cross parcels. This is quite true: it would be impossible to save anything like sufficient food to keep one from being hungry.

Relativity

But, most old Kriegies who have at one time or another been without Red Cross food, will admit that this business of belting is all a matter of relativity. An extra biscuit now, when we have enough, seems to be as nothing, but when you haven't had a biscuit for days and your stomach is flapping up against your back-bone, believe the old Kriegies, that extra biscuit becomes a banquet.

Hoard Gash

The same theory applies to milk, sugar, fat and any little bits of gash. When you have nothing but German rations to live on it is really quite amazing what can be done with these little extras.

To illustrate this improvisation a member of the *Recco* staff can well remember baking a Vinegar Stalag Pie. This consisted of potatoes cooked in a tin in ashes. Baked without fat, but with vinegar added to taste. And at the time it tasted wizard.

Belt Box

References to the Belt Box were also made at the Mess Meeting. There is no finer institution than the belt box. A few bits of gash dropped into it in times of plenty look like whole Red Cross parcels (well almost) when the belt is on us. As Sgt. Sands pointed out, it may never happen but it is foolish not to be prepared when precautionary measures are so simple.

It was about this time too that the War started coming nearer to us. Our issue of March 11 carried the story of attacks in the vicinity of our former home at Barth on the edge of the Baltic:

BARTH IN ACTION ZONE
NEW ARRIVALS SEE BLITZED TOWNS

The seven men who came into the camp from Barth yesterday morning brought the following news:

The Camp leader is Wing Commander Hilton;

strength is now about 2,000 increasing weekly.

There are four Lagers.

The newcomers report there are about three air raid alarms daily. Aircraft are rarely seen but the noise of machine-guns and cannons can be heard.

A .5 machine gun link was picked up in the camp.

On a night raid on Berlin, it took British bombers three quarters of an hour to pass over the camp.

On their way to this camp they passed through heavily damaged towns. At Stettin the factory area and the works is badly damaged and at Marienberg there is also severe damage and the bridge over the river is demolished.

The seven men confirmed the report of a new RAF camp at Marienberg and they stopped for a night at a Canadian camp at Stargard. This camp, which is very well built, has concrete roads: the prisoners are Dieppe boys.

At Barth there has been a recent outbreak of meningitis with one fatality – Lieutenant Thomas.

The camp is also reported to be infested with crabs.

On the 30th of the month we carried another story of interest to every member of the camp – for we had all come through the interrogation centre at Dulag Luft on the outskirts of Frankfurt-am-Main.

DULAG BLITZED

Yesterday's party of forty new arrivals stated that Frankfurt is badly damaged and the town edge camp of Dulag is flattened and gutted by fire.

On Wednesday night, 15th March, eight days before the party left, the RAF raided Frankfurt and left it burning. On Saturday the town was raided again and on the following Wednesday before the party left, the ruins received a daylight attack by American bombers and at night another RAF raid. During this raid half of the party was in the railway siding when it escaped harm amongst the ruins of burning rolling stock. The remainder were in a six feet deep air-raid shelter when a 4,000lb and another of smaller calibre dropped within 40 yards of them.

The bombs wrecked the camp, destroying 6,000 parcels and a large reserve of clothing. One man in the shelter was killed. He was an American officer who was knocked over by the concussion and struck his head, receiving fatal injuries.

Three other men were wounded.

It was later discovered that a stick of dud bombs had been dropped across the camp.

At the same time as we were publishing these items of purely local interest involving fellow prisoners travelling across Germany in our usual *40 Hommes/8 Chevaux* style we carried, almost daily, items relating to the war in general – as we knew it – and in particular developments on the Russian front. Each barracks had a map of Russia and countless pundits who were, according to them, masters of tactics and strategy. Some of them, I feel, made their reputations simply on the ability to pronounce the tongue-twisting Russian names which figured in the daily German radio and press reports.

In another camp in another time, the relentless German advance across Russia had brought gloom and despondency. Now each German retreat, whether classified as a strategic withdrawal or not, brought a corresponding lift to the Kriegie spirit. It was only when we saw some of the Russian prisoners that we doubted whether their advances would be long-lasting. For the men we saw were ill-clad and pathetic – even taking into account the fact that they had reached our part of Germany from whatever part of Russia – on foot.

Verboten

At Sagan the censor's blue pencil took the shape of an axe which chopped down quite brutally. It was a simple case of no more publication . . . *Verboten, nicht mehr, kaput.*

At Heydekrug the process was more subtle. The *Recco* was banned shortly after we reported that because of the bomb-damaged state of Berlin we could no longer hire theatrical costumes from the German capital. At the same time we commented that the embargo on costumes brought no great problems because, in future, the costumes used in our plays and revues would be entirely made from British materials and by British craftsmen and that meant best. We pointed out as proof that the glamorous dress worn by Roy Dotrice who later went on to win fame and fortune on the London stage, had been made from a tattered Canadian shirt, plus a piece of the inevitable gash material. The article No More Berlin Costumes appeared to have caught the eye of the goons who queued with the prisoners to read our daily offerings. They must have been even more offended two days later when we carried an article headed, The U-boat Menace.

Publication was stopped. It was resumed twelve days later after an appeal from Dixie Deans to the Kommandant – but strictly on the proviso that, in future, all editions would first have to pass the German censor. Reluctantly we agreed to comply, believing that the *Recco* had become such a necessary institution that the camp would be worse off without it– despite the restrictions that blue-pencilling implied. From then on the *Recco* carried, beside its title, a *Gepüft* or censorship stamp, the first being applied on issue 61, dated April 20, 1944.

In issue 69 dated May 1, 1944, the *Recco* made its last public appearance, carrying two items calculated not to endear us to our German captors. The first revealed that six of our numbers had been arrested by the Germans.

SIX ARRESTED PENDING CHARGE

On Saturday afternoon the following NCOs were taken into protective custody by the Germans:

Morris, Potter, Snowdon, Webster, Wood and Barnes.

Issue 61 in the Heydekrug camp near the Lithuanian border was the first to require the camp authorities' *geprüft* stamp. As the atmosphere became more tense with the development of the war, it proved to be one of the last editions of the *Daily Recco*

Daily Recco

Issue no 61

"Freedom and Boar"

Rollcall 0900 and 1700

Thursday 20th April 1944

German Radio

The German radio yesterday reported that:

"St5ong American bomber formations yesterday attacked the BERLIN area. They brought with them strong fighter support. Damage and casualties were caused in RATENAU. German fighters and Flak, despite difficult defence conditions shot down 44 a/c, 40 of which were 4-engined bombers.

Last night strong formations of German heavy bombers attacked targets in LONDON. Large fires and great damage resulted. Other German a/c attacked targets in E. England.

In the SEBASTOPOL area strong Soviet attacks supported by artillery and battle a/c were repulsed by the German defences.

On the Lower DNIESTER numerous Soviet attacks were repulsed and local breaches blocked or barred off.

N. of JASSY strong Soviet attacks were again repulsed.

Between the Carpathians and E. of STANISLAW German and Hungarian troops continued their attacks successfully and retook the town of NADWORNA from the Soviets.

The Soviet lines S. of the DNIESTER were pushed further back by the Soviet attacks.

Repeated Soviet attacks S.W. of LUZK and W. of TARNOPOL failed.

In Italy on the NETTUNO beach-head and S. of the Adriatic coast all enemy thrusts were repulsed with high losses.

Softball to take Advantage of Dry weather

At a recently held meeting of the Softball committee it was decided thatnthere would be 9 teams in the Major league, 10 teams in the Minor league and that each room should field a team in the Barrack league.

The schedule for the Barrack league is rooms in A Block versus B Block and C versus D, winners to play off. This means some 380 fixtures of which 7 to 10 would be played off each day during the summer.

W/O Bartlam who is the ottee. member for the Barrack league stated that all plans are ready to be put into action. During the summer each team will be playing every three or four days.

He added that at present teams must be limited to one per room but plans are under way for expansion subject to circumstances.

Arrangements are being made for the tuition of scorers under Col. Boong, the Barrack league official scorer and record keeper.

Arrangements for starting have been made with the Rugby and Football ottee., who will allow the pitch to be used for softball during rugby time on Tuesday and Friday afternoons from 12.30 to 5.00pm.

The Soccer ottee's decision on time allowed during soccer periods on the pitch is not yet forthcoming.

The leagues will commence as soon as regular times on the pitch are secured.

Incomplete Mail

The following letters and cards are at present in the Camp Office with the Absender details incomplete.

Miss P. Barnett, Ottawa.
Signed Kenny.
Miss Daphne King, London.
Signed Dave.
MIss B. Neehan, Aberystwyth.
Signed Alex.
Miss A. Wylie, Vancouver.
Signed Charlie.
Mr. O.R. Smith, Hanwell.
Signed Bob.
Miss J. Cave, Victoria, B.C.
Signed Lee?
Miss Mona Daughtery, Bidstone, Cheshire.
Signed Les.
Rev. G. Biddle, Victoria.
Signed Cecil.
Miss Peggy Clarke, Stonehouse Glous.
Signed Jack.

World Press News

During the last German air raid on London a depot with over one million books intended for British Servicemen overseas was hit and burned out.

According to the "Manchester Guardian" New Zealand in proportion to her population has suffered the heaviest losses in this war. On the population count as a basis, she has at least twice as many dead as Australia and five times as many as Canada.

The Admiralty announces the loss of 413 officers and men dead and wounded out of the ship's complement of 450 of the cruiser H.M.S. Penelope.

Reuter reports that Wall Str. financiers reckon the coming invasion will cost 100 milliard dollars.

Football Meeting

There will be a meeting of the Football ottee. at 7.45pm prompt in the Sports store to-night.

All room reps. are requested to attend.

The business will be the election of a new president as the present president Jimmy Bryce is intending to transfer to K Lager.

Wanted

Wanted new shaving brush in exchange for 200 cigarettes and 3 tins of tobacco. Similar quantity offered for a pair of nail-scissors
GREEN   A 8.

Wanted size 10 or 9½ shoes for a pair size 9.
STEPHENSON D 8.

Wanted drying cloths for cigarettes.
MURRAY   B 9.

Wanted pair of new good quality plimsoles, size large 9 for similar pair hard-court soles, size small 9,
MAHONEY   A 10.

Wanted size 7 gym. shoes or canvas boots for size 7 leather sandals.
GREAGER, CAMP OFF.

Lost

Lost one R.A.F. tunic with wrist-watch and metal bracelet in pocket. Red triangle on back of tunic. Please return to:
SCZEPANOWSKI   A 2.

M E N U

All Camp - Biscuit special.

A,C,D - Bully & potatoes.
B Block - Bully fritters.

Mackay-Whitlock Press

The last-named is Camp Secretary in K Lager.

No reasons for the detention have so far been given by the authorities.

And immediately below we carried, in a black-bordered box, a report of the funeral of T/Sgt. Walker who had been killed attempting to escape:

The funeral of T/Sgt Walker who was killed while attempting to escape in the early hours of Saturday morning, took place at 15.00 hours yesterday.

Sgt. Deans who attended the Memorial Service in E Lager, conducted by Padres Morton and Jackson, was refused permission to go to the graveside.

The Drs. were also refused permission to attend.

T/Sgt Walker's body, wrapped in a blanket and covered by the stars and Stripes, was lowered into a bough-covered grave. Padre Morgan gave the address at the graveside.

A wreath of paper flowers was sent from this compound bearing the inscription In proud memory from comrades in the Royal Air Force.

For the Germans that appeared to be the last straw. The blue pencil again turned into an axe and so, on Labour Day, our labours ceased . . . and there were, according to our banner, still 239 days to Christmas.

Office B9

Wires MacLock

239 Days

Nation-wide Ho

Bournemouth Bulletin

Great excitement in Feb. when lemons came to the town for the first time since goodness knows when. Allocation was one pound per customer: hundreds were unlucky. Oranges are coming through fairly frequently now.

Bournemouth's youngsters are hot stuff at identifying a/c. In the Southern Region's team which won National Aircraft Recognition Trophy, seven of the eight members were Bournemouth lads.

Laughter occurred in Court when, giving evidence concerning the showing of a light in the blackout a policeman said, "When I spoke to defendant he said it must have been his wife who left the lights on. Just then his wife came in – he said nothing".

Youth had its say at the Municipal College when 300 attended a conference "Youth looks ahead". They made it clear to the local bigwigs that they want more say in the government of the town and that the men who come back from fighting must be allowed more opportunity for taking part in its administration. They said there must be no question of preferential treatment for the monied classes.

Post-war plans for Bournemouth include a suggestion from a local estate agent that it should capitalise its proximity to the continent by running a passenger speed-boat service. R.A.F. rescue launches and invasion craft to be used.

Murde

One mo Brussels' facto known faces wer

The three hu attention to th ers", of whom t bout forty.

BUZZER AS

At 8.15am., the buzzer soun work, the forty revolvers and g forced the majo employees into

Several work another floor i ing, knew nothi hold-up until i over.

MASKED L

The leader o who was masked, centre of the r four of his acc forced the cash the safe.

During this of the gang wh control of the building, cutta wires.

COURTESY

The bandits two cars, takin one of the firs which was found the day. They one and a half francs. The ne sent back a po

The last straw – after the items in the issue of May 1, 1944, the *Daily Recco* was axed by the German captors

Daily Recco

Issue 69

ristmas   "Freedom and Boat"   Roll Call 0800 and 1700   Monday 1st May 1944

-ups Sweep
elgium
Every-day Affairs"

ast month when employees of a trooping into work, a few un-ed.

mployees of the form paid little

rang-re a-longing to one of the clerk which they had borrowed and which contained the clerk's sandwiches and tobacco. Enclosed in the portfolio when was a card "Avec nos Excuse start ok put and the ms.

PRUDENT POLICE

A witness managed to warn the police, but was sy on told that there were no pol-uild-icemen at hand.
he   It is reported that one ll policeman did timidly poke a white helmet round the corner, but drew back pre-ang, cipitately. He has not been in th seen nor heard of since.
le

WILD WEST
s
open   Organises thefts of this type are reported to be commonplace, and in many e res cases larger sums - ten ined million francs at a time -the are stolen from Banks.
phone   Murders, also common, are mostly for political reasons. Reprisals are al-in ways taken by the opposite them party.
ies
in
ut

Raffle
hey
be-   The raffle for the box of cigars was won by Sgt.

Six Arrested Pending Charge

On Saturday afternoon the following N.C.O's were taken into "protective custody" by the Germans.
MORRIS, POTTER, SNOWDON, WEBSTER, WOOD and BARNES.
The last-named is camp secretary in K Lager.
No reasons for the detention have so far been given by the authorities.

The funeral of T/Sgt Walker, who was killed while attempting to escape in the early hours of Saturday morning, took place at 15.00 hours yesterday.
Sgt. Deans, who attended the Memorial Service in E Lager, conducted by Padres Morton and Jackson, was refused permission to go to the graveside. The Drs. were also refused permission to attend.
T/Sgt. Walker's body, wrapped in a blanket and covered by the Stars and Stripes, was lowered into a bough-covered grave. Padre Morgan gave the Address at the graveside.
A wreath of paper flowers was sent from this compound bearing the inscription "In proud memory from comrades in the Royal Air Forces".

The inter-compound soccer game - England vs. Scotland which was postponed last Sunday, will take place in K Lager to-day.

American Raid On Berlin

The German radio reported yesterday that:
"American bomber formations yesterday attacked BERLIN under the cover of thick cloud. The residential areas suffered damage and the population losses. 129 a/c were shot down by the German air defences, 121 of which were 4-motored bombers.
Last night British bombers attacked the Lower RHINE area.
Large scale attacks were carried out last night on PLYMOUTH and shipping concentrations on the S.W. coast by forces of German heavy bombers.
During a raid on TOULON 15 enemy a/c were shot down.
Low-flying enemy a/c bombed and machine-gunned a German Red Cross hospital in ITALY.
Soviet attacks in the SEBASTOPOL area and on the Lower DNIESTER were of a local character and were unsuccessful.
A counter-attack by German and Rumanian forces strongly supported by battle a/c was completely successful in the battle area of JASSY. 14 tanks, 30 guns and other war material was either destroyed or fell into German hands.
Despite stubborn Soviet resistance, the German-Hungarian attacking forces gained further ground between the CARPATHIANS and the Upper DNIESTER. Strong Soviet counter-attacks were repulsed by the Hungarian troops.
Repeated Soviet attacks E. of POLOZK were unsuccessful.
A strongly protected Russian convoy on the BLACK SEA was attacked by a German U-boat.

Chess Solution

KEY MOVE: B-KB8.
1.B-KB8,   XXXX.P-K5.
2.R-K7,   BxR.
3.BxB,   P-K6.
4.Kt-QB3,   MATE.
1.B-KB8,   P-K5.
2.R-K7,   P-K6.
3.R-K4,   P-K7.
4.RxB,   MATE.
1.B-KB8,   BxB.
2.Kt-QB3Ch.,K-QR6.
3.R-QKt3,   MATE.
1.B-KB8,   B-QR4.
2.R-QB7,   BxR.
3.Kt-QB3,   MATE.
1.B-KB8,   B-QR4.
2.R-QB7, B or P moves.
3.R-Qb4Ch.,   B-Kt5.
4.RxB,   MATE.

Wanted

Wanted shoes or gym. shoes or canvas boots size 9, for new pair football boots size 10.
DAVIS   C 3.

Wanted good pair of pyjamas, new preferred, for cigarettes.
RECCO   OFFICE.

Wanted chocolate or brews for Van Heusen shirts and collars, size 15.
RECCO   OFFICE.

Wanted a copy of "Physical and Dynamical Met" by Brunt. Will anyone who has or who knows of a copy please see   BOOTH   A 8.

Lost

Lost a copy of "The song of a Sourdough" by Robert Service. Please return to Padre MORGAN.

STOP   PRESS

MACKAY-WHITLOCK

PRESS

Freedom and Boat

After the *Recco* closed in the summer of '44, we moved to Fallingbostel, near the town of Celle and a very short distance from the concentration camp at Belsen. For months our new camp seethed with rumours. Rumours about the end of the war. Rumours about what the Germans would do. Rumours about what would happen to us. There seemed only one certainty – the end of the war was near. The Kriegies' longed-for Home for Christmas was coming. It would be welcomed – no matter what month it was.

Now it was March 1945. Overflying of the camp by Allied planes was an almost daily occurrence. From following the course of the War on maps of faraway Russia, we were following the campaigns on the map of Europe and even Germany itself.

We were told that, end of the war or not, we were to be moved again. It appeared that the Germans were to use us as bargaining pieces with whatever advancing army reached us first. But we were not going to be left in the camp to await deliverance. We were told we had to move . . . but this time it was not to be by train, even as substitute *8 Chevaux*. This time it was to be on foot and we could take only what we could carry on our backs, in our hands or wherever.

Designs for haversacks were dreamed up, manufactured – and discarded. Smaller, slim-line, more sensible packs were devised – and discarded. Blankets were stitched together in squares, oblongs and triangles. Red Cross string was plaited into ropes so that the loosely-made haversacks could be loosely humped over thin shoulders. Sharing of ideas, designs and blatant imitation became the order of the day as the prisoners worked like beavers to fashion receptacles into which they could stack essentials of food and clothing and whatever treasures, amassed during the years of captivity, they felt they could not live without. I took the copies of the *Recco* with me.

Barrack by barrack the prisoners moved out of the camp over the period of a few days. When our turn came we stepped off blithely. We knew that at the end of the march lay only one thing – freedom. The guards, with a different fate awaiting them, were edgy, bad-tempered and violent. The least step out of line brought the barrel of a machine-pistol crashing down on to unprotected bodies. The thump of marching boots was interspersed with the click of guns being cocked. The prisoners, who had survived being shot down and captured and then the years of imprisonment, fell back into line. After surviving so much for so long there was no point in risking it all now.

Our march took us east, west, north and south, marching in the opposite direction to the British, American and Russian armies. When we marched east we found the roads blocked by fleeing German civilians – with haversacks like ours – and with wooden handcarts piled high with domestic belongings.

Ivan, Ivan, they cried, looking fearfully over their shoulders.

We reckoned that with the way they had treated their Russian prisoners over the years, they had every right to look fearful.

Our column trudged on.

At nights we settled in the yard of some poor farmer – certainly poorer by the next morning when he surveyed what was left of his livestock. Prisoners could put locusts to shame, removing potatoes, turnips, eggs and even chickens under the noses of farmers and guards in so many seconds. The liberated fowls were then plucked inside home-made sleeping bags to minimise the signalling of retribution by floating, windblown feathers. The prisoners lived well, if dangerously; the farmers aged visibly and cursed volubly and took even tighter precautions to guard their produce and livestock before the arrival of the next column of marching Kriegies.

So we marched, day by day, east, west, north, south. We passed Belsen and saw the thin scarecrow inmates in their distinctive striped uniforms shambling on the inside of the wire. We knew how they felt – up to a point. One day our marching column was halted at noon. A lorry arrived carrying Red Cross parcels. They were shared out and attacked – voraciously. Taking advantage of the parcel issue, the Germans refused to issue our daily eighth of a loaf. No problem. We spread peanut butter on either slices of Spam or cheese. It tasted well. But the following day the exotic meal took its toll. Millie, my second pilot, had to be left, squatting at the roadside passing blood. He would be picked up later and taken to hospital with other prisoners who, for one reason or another, could not continue.

We trudged on, passing dead and bloated cows and horses at the side of the road, innocent victims of the cannon and machine-gun fire from the Allied fighter planes which had been strafing retreating German troops. But they were not all German troops that were attacked. One day as we marched northwards, we met another column of Kriegies – marching south. They had left Fallingbostel two days before us and were now headed back to where we had been. But the joking about the craziness of the situation was soon stilled. The other Kriegies told us that, the previous day, many of them had been killed. American fighter pilots, mistaking them for a German platoon, had strafed them with cannon fire. The dead, who had survived being shot down in their own kites, had survived the bitter years of incarceration and all the ills of imprisonment, had been killed by friendly action. Bitterness about the futile waste of life rose like bile in our throats.

Planes – our planes – and gunfire became more common. The war – and liberation – were definitely coming nearer. But we continued to march round and round in ever-decreasing circles – our home-made haversacks, despite becoming lighter as food stocks disappeared along with treasures whose weight had made them appear less and less valuable, irked our shoulders. I decided that the bundles of the *Daily Recco* would have to go. But editorial pride and a parent's love of the first-born ruled against just dumping them in a ditch or scattering them to the four winds. But where could they go that would be safe so I could return later to retrieve them?

The answer came that night. Since Millie had dropped out of the march I had chummed up with Chan – Bernard Channing who had been on our squadron and who, joining our combine in camp, had kept us amused – and intrigued – by the clocks he made from old tins. That night, while Chan chatted up a guard, I sidled round to the door of the farmhouse to see what I could get from the farmer in the way of milk and eggs in exchange for cigarettes and our last half bar of chocolate. But instead of an angry, harassed and suspicious farmer, the door was opened by a middle-aged woman who spoke English. She agreed to a barter and then, in a flood of words unleashed by the chance to speak English again, she revealed that

she was a South African; that she had come to Germany in the summer of
'39 and had been unable to return to her homeland. She agreed that war
was terrible; that the end of the war was near and added that at the first
opportunity, she would be on her way back to South Africa.

I decided to take a chance. Would she, I asked, look after some papers for
me? Would she keep them for just a few days until the Allied armies
arrived when I would return to collect them? Friendly as she had been, she
suddenly became frightened, really frightened. Obviously conversation
with a young pilot was one thing, but to do something positive to help a
Prisoner of War was another. I explained what the papers were and that
they carried censorship stamps so that clearly they were not anything
subversive for her to worry about. I was not trying to conceal them from
the guards – all I wanted was to get rid of the weight out of my haversack –
at the same time trying to preserve the *Recco*s as a record of camp life.
Eventually she agreed to keep them safe and dry until my return. I trusted
her. And while Chan passed more cigarettes to the by now friendly guard, I
returned to my sleeping bag, took the *Recco*s from the haversack and
handed them over to the *Hausfrau*. I also gave her my home address.

The next morning we set off on the march again. My pack was lighter and
it was May Day. But it was snowing. We felt miserable.

During the night Chan and I had decided that 'enough was enough'. We
would make a break for it at the first opportunity and try to reach the lines
of the British or the Americans – whichever was nearer. Our opportunity
came in mid-morning. American fighter planes roared in from the south.
Our column from the air must have looked like a very ragged *Wehrmacht*
company. The planes' cannons opened up. Without waiting to see what the
guards were doing Chan and I led the dash of Kriegies into a roadside
copse. While our mates flattened themselves out under the trees we kept on
running. A third set of footsteps crashed after us. We waited for the
challenge and the bullet. None came. Risking a glance backwards we saw
that fellow Kriegie Jimmy Upham had decided to follow us. Huddled in a
shallow hollow and with no sign of our marching companions or the
guards, we told Jimmy that we thought the British forces were only one
day's march to the west and that was where we were aiming. He opted to
join us.

For over two hours we lay there, listening for the sound of searching and pursuit. None came. We came to the edge of the copse and found another road. It was deserted and on the far side was another wood. But in a clearing right at the edge we could see German half-tracks, lorries and staff cars. We cursed. But there was no sight nor sound of activity. The vehicles were deserted – abandoned. We lay and watched and waited. After what seemed hours of utter silence we dashed across the road into the clearing and crouched beside one of the staff cars, an open-topped Mercedes. The only sound we heard was the pumping of blood in our temples. The staff car, in the mottled camouflage of the German army, had petrol in it. We could hear it sloshing about when we rocked the vehicle. But it had no ignition keys. Chan, a motor mechanic back in civvy street, grabbed under the dashboard, pulled some wires, twisted them together and the engine started. We were in business.

Jimmy Upham confessed that he could not drive and Chan volunteered the information that he was an expert – on motorbikes only. My own driving experience was slight – along with three mates at Filton I had shared ownership and driving of an Austin Swallow – at least I knew how to operate the Merc's gears. Or so I thought. The gears crashed, the engine almost stalled. Then with a roar, the car kangarooed forward out of the clearing on to the roadway. We headed west. We were like three kids on a Sunday School outing – kids whose cocoa had been laced with rum. We sang, we joked, we cheered, we waved to bushes and empty fields. Unused to the power of the Mercedes, I took a sharp bend too fast and skidded. The brakes squealed as we drew to halt – right under the nose of a tank, its gun muzzle almost touching our bonnet. No driving manual I had ever read told the reader what to do when turning a corner and being met by a tank. The gun muzzle dipped. A hedge of sten guns advanced on either side of the tank. They were held rock-firm by khaki clad figures wearing the shoulder flashes of the Brigade of Guards. We're British we yelled. Out! said an unsmiling tank commander. We outed.

Later, after the soldiers had searched us and the car, we were led before the tank commander. Our story had been accepted, but, regretfully, he said, he could not go to the rescue of our mates we had left half a day earlier when we ducked out of the column. He had outrun his supplies and the rest of the British troops advancing in that sector. But gallantly he provided us with cigarettes, hard tack and instructions on how to find our way through the British lines and on to the road to Brussels. Gaily we set off to follow the square route south signs hammered on to trees at the side of the road. Lustily we sang, an operation made difficult and less tuneful because our mouths were full of army-provided chocolate. Going back to the farm and the South African *Hausfrau* was forgotten. We were on our way to Brussels – and home.

While we took a breather at a crossroads a convoy of half a dozen vehicles rolled up. Germans. So much for our liberty, we thought, praying that the grey-clad troops would think only of taking us prisoner again. One of their officers approached. We surrender he said. We blinked. We need benzine – and guns we said. The whole German convoy obliged, divesting themselves of hand guns and holsters, machine-pistols, rifles. We then directed them up the road we had come – straight into the arms of the Guards armoured division soldiers we had left not so long ago. Taking a souvenir Luger each, we left the pile of arms at the roadside and continued following the signposts south.

A couple of hours later we found, as we had been told by the Guards armoured boys, a Service Corps depot. We stopped. We tasted our first white bread for four years. It's just like cake said Chan. Our car was filled to the brim with tins of beef, beans, peaches and loaves, the tank was filled with petrol and with two cartons of cigarettes each we drove out of the depot on the road to Brussels once again. We had a puncture. Within minutes the Service Corps boys had the wheel off the car, the ripped inner tube replaced with a jeep inner tube and the wheel back on again. We felt like royalty. But in our ears rang the warning of the Service Corps men – "You'll have trouble crossing the Rhine."

As we drove south we found, indeed, that bridges were in somewhat short supply over the river. But at Emmerich we found one, still standing and still in use. But a far-from-friendly soldier standing guard at our end of the bridge notified us testily that only convoys were being allowed to cross and that no exception could be taken for three men in a hotchpotch of uniforms, unhatted and unshaven, and whose language was difficult to understand because they never stopped eating. We pleaded. The guard refused to listen. We turned back. We stopped half a mile down the road and watched as convoy after convoy crawled to the summit of a small hill before easing down to the bridge. Just after dark as yet another convoy neared the top of the hill one of the drivers missed his gears and stalled. We slid into the space and rolled down – and over – the bridge. But now that we were in a convoy there was no way of getting out until they decided to stop. Stop they did – at another Service Corps depot. Our tale of prison camp life, the march and our escape from it earned us a free bed for the night, supper and another load of provisions to be loaded into our car which by now was starting to resemble a travelling shop.

The next morning we drove south – again. In Niemegen a Dutch civilian stepped into the middle of the road to stop our car. The war is over, he yelled. Please come with me and be my guests. We went. It was our first taste of home cooking for four years. It was wonderful. From the car we unloaded supplies and took them in to our Dutch host, his wife and family. It was like Christmas. The next day, after tearful and joyful farewells, we continued towards Brussels. In Antwerp we stopped in the street beside a young British soldier and asked, would you please buy us some ice-cream? He looked in amazement, first at us and then at our car, weighing in his mind the peculiar reason for three tramps in a German staff car not having a sou to their name. When we explained he obliged. We sat back in the Merc and licked our wafers – heaven must be something like this.

We knew we were in Brussels by the cobbles. Rapidly we made a plan of campaign. We would flog the car for as much as we could get from the first crooked-looking character that we came upon. The city appeared to be full of them. We chose a flashily-dressed youngish man holding up the doorway of a little café in one of the suburbs. I wiped the rust off my schooldays French and propositioned him. What happened next was like something out of a low-grade gangster movie. After a good deal of haggling and two lung-exploding Gauloises in the car supplied by our new-found friend who clearly recognised a bargain when he sat in one, the Belgian led me into the café – and straight into the lavatory. Pulling out a bulging wallet, he peeled off the equivalent of £150 English in large white Belgian notes to seal the deal which involved the immediate removal of the car for respraying to get rid of the German camouflage. He bought me a *Fine* at the cafe bar. I told him he could keep the piles of food which had been keeping Jimmy Upham company in the spacious rear seat.

Back outside I told Chan and Jimmy that they were now millionaires – that we had enough money to give us a good night out on the town before surrendering to authority with a polite request to Please Take Us Home. We emptied the car of our personal belongings and went into the café. The patron, noticing the bundles of notes we each had, put a full bottle of cognac on the counter. Eventually, in a kind of haze from which we never managed fully to escape for the next twenty four hours, we left the café and hitched a lift to the centre of Brussels. We wandered around in open-eyed amazement, gazing at shop windows full of luxury items, the like of which we had not seen even in pre-War London. We bought perfume, silk scarves and chocolates to take home. We bought wine and brandy to be consumed on the premises. We found, and ignored, the Malcolm Club where off-duty airmen were being lodged and fed at cut-rate prices, thanks to the generosity of the mother of the dead flyer whose name gave the club its title. We wandered around the city centre in a hazy daze, marking, for future reference, a military transit centre from which, without going in, we had learned that we could be repatriated.

But first things first. We were determined to enjoy new-found freedom – and wealth. But, plastered as we became, we kept the transit centre at the centre of our wanderings. It was the pivot around which we revolved – literally. One thing we discovered, and there were tentative proposals that we should use our back pay turning our knowledge into a business, was that in direct ratio to the amount of wine and brandy we consumed, our French became progressively more fluent – the Stalag School of Languages – centred in a vineyard of course – had a fine ring to it.

Somewhere in the night Jimmy and I lost Chan. We retraced – albeit with difficulty – our footsteps to the last bar where he had positively been in our company. It was the one where we both remembered Chan complaining bitterly to the patron that while we were willing to spend money in his rotten dump he should have the graciousness to remain open. The patron had not seen it that way. Chan could not be found. Jimmy and I sought solace in the bars that were still open. Then, at six o'clock in the morning, we went to the transit centre. The figure asleep on the doorstep was Chan.

How Many Days to Christmas?

Deloused and almost humanised, along with another group of former Kriegies, we were driven from the transit centre to the airport, loaded on to an RAF transport plane and flown home to Blighty. It was at the moment of crossing the English coast that I appreciated everything they had to say about the white cliffs of Dover. Kitted out in new uniforms, we were debriefed on our prison camp experiences and how we came to be shot down all those years ago. I wondered if I was to be told that the cost of another Wimpy was to be deducted from my pay.

We were fed and paid and sent home.

Shortly after my return to Broughty Ferry, my late cousin Arthur Neave, a civilian lawyer and at that time a Captain in the Army Legal Department, came to see me. He revealed that he was to take part in the Nuremberg war crimes trials – defending some of the Nazi hierarchy, an action none to his liking, but being carried out as part of his duties. He said he would be stationed in or around Nuremberg – not too far from Bleckmar and the farm where I had left the *Reccos*. Giving him directions as best I could, I asked if he would take a trip there, trace my South African *Hausfrau* and see if, hope beyond hope, she had indeed hung on to and preserved the *Reccos*. Arthur said, war crimes duties permitting, he would do what he could.

He was as good as his word. On his next leave home three months later, he turned up complete with the *Reccos* still tied in their original bundles.

And just two months after that I received a letter from the displaced persons camp at Bridge of Weir near Glasgow. It was from my South African benefactress whose action in preserving the *Reccos* and handing them over to my cousin had earned her a faster than usual return home to Africa with the Bridge of Weir camp a staging post on the journey. I drove through to meet her, had afternoon tea with her in the camp which was vaguely reminiscent of a real Prisoner of War camp and gave her a present and good wishes for the rest of her journey home. I have not heard from her since nor she from me.

Basic pay for Alan Mackay was 11/6 (57½p per day), later increased to 17/6 (87½p per day). Alan Mackay's RAF Airman's Pay Book shows backpayment and due to his years in prison, he arrived home to a nest egg of over £700 – a fortune in 1945, but still not worth it!

3										4		
DAILY RATES							**OF PAY**					
Promotions, Reductions, Reclassifications and							Remusterings, and Alterations in Allotment.					
RATES OF			TOTAL	DEDUCT			NET RATE ISSUABLE		*Date from which NET RATE OF PAY is issuable	*Reason for change in Net Rate (e.g., Promotions, Reductions Alterations in Allotments, etc.)		Officer's Signature, Station and Date
Consolidated Pay	Good Conduct Pay	Qualification Pay		Allotments and/or Compulsory Stoppage	Income Tax	P.O.S.B. Deposits.	Figures	Words				
				weekly			*Weekly*					
11/6	.	WS1 2/6	20/.	√2/.	33/1		92/11	Nineteen Shillings	Two Elevenpence			10b√RC Cosford Cape 1/6
17/6	·/3·	2/6	20/3	√2/-	33/1.		94/8	ninety four sh.	Eightpence	Award of G.C.B W.E.F. 2/9/42:		b/c PRC 8/8/45 Cape 1/6
17/6	·/3	3/-	20/9	√2/.	.1.17.6		4/9	four sh. nine pence	3.5.41	WS1 for 6 yrs		1/5 PRC 30.11.44

Temporary emoluments, e.g., Duty Pay, Ration Allowance, etc., should be shown on page 2, not on pages 3 and 4.

* Where a change occurs in the net rate of pay, the officer making the entry is, in addition to making the appropriate entries above, to write across the columns for Cash Payments (pages 5 to 9) the amended net rate of pay and the effective date. Temporary stoppages of pay are to be recorded only on pages 5 to 9. (See note on page 5.)

The *Daily Recco*s, read avidly by my family, were bound in two volumes – the handwritten and the typewritten – and forgotten. They would probably still be in my garage gathering still more dampness, had not Jack Garret, the New Zealand POW leader in our camps, made his trip to Scotland. Thanks to his insistence, the interest shown in the volumes by members of the Royal Air Forces ex-Prisoners of War Association in London and the tolerance of my wife Margaret who has had to suffer the lengthy gestation period taken to bring *313 Days to Christmas* to life, these daily accounts of Prisoner of War life are now available to be read by ex-Kriegies and by a whole new generation who, hopefully, will never learn at first hand what war and prison camp life can be like.

The originals, already on microfilm at the Royal Air Force Museum at Hendon, will hopefully be of some use in helping the memories of ex-Kriegies who used to stand, bleary-eyed, reading the *Daily Recco* and learning, if nothing else, how many days there were to Christmas.

Glossary

Abwehr

German security forces.

Achtung

Watch out. A warning supposed to be shouted by guards at prisoners if they got too near the warning wire – a single knee-high strand within a few feet of the double-banked barbed wire which enclosed each camp compound. At certain stages of the war – at the beginning when they were superconfident; in the middle when troops injured on the Russian front were drafted in as guards; and at the end when bitterness crept in with the realisation that Hitler was failing to fulfil their dreams – the guards were trigger happy and generally fired before shouting 'Achtung'. On the other hand prisoners used to tempt fate by seeing how far they could go, allegedly in search of a ball, before alerting the guards in the watch towers spaced all round the perimeter of the camp.

Appell

Rollcall. The twice-daily ritual of the Germans counting the heads of all prisoners in the camp. The Germans were not noted for their counting ability with the result that Appells stretched interminably. The counting, two at a time, could also be delayed by the Kriegies playing games with the guards making the count. By this means the guards ended up with a total far in excess of the number of prisoners in the camp. Other prisoners played billiards, table tennis, cricket etc, in mime at the rear of the ranks . . . a practice which greatly annoyed the guards at the same time as bringing some light relief to the bored ranks waiting to be counted.

During really bad weather Appells were held within the huts. Because of the overcrowding of beds, tables, etc, this was a highly complicated procedure for the Germans. As a result they held as many Apells out in the open as possible . . . in the rain and snow rather than be mucked about by the prisoners in the confines of the barracks.

Arbeit

Work. The German slogan *Kein Arbeit, Kein Brot,* meaning no work – no bread, was answered by the prisoners' slogan of 'No bread – no work'. This brought about, generally, stalemate as opposed to stale bread.

barracks

Wooden huts which prisoners, with amazing ingenuity, turned into home.
Filled with two-tiered bunks, tables and benches, the huts quickly developed personalities and inter-barrack rivalry in sport, etc, was high. The bunks had wooden slat bases and straw or wood shaving filled palliasses. In hard winters the slats were used as fuel, resulting in prisoners lying on mattresses which undulated between the remaining slats.

blower

Highly-efficient Heath Robinsonish hand-operated fire box. Made out of old Red Cross tins on a wooden frame plus a lot of ingenuity, the blowers made the maximum use of the minimum fuel – and so helped to save the bed boards.

Brot

Bread. The German black bread was entirely foreign

to the prisoners' palates. Issued in 2lb loaves, the bread was rationed in portions of a half, seventh, eighth or even less according to the state of the war and the German supplies.

Frequently hard and teeth-breaking, it was even known to knock a man out.

combine

A group of two or more prisoners who in a cooperative system shared practically everything. Especially useful when Red Cross parcels, ideally one per man per week, were in short supply and sometimes issued at the rate of one parcel between eight.

Deutsch

German. Generally used as an adjective followed by the noun bastards.

Dulag Luft

The initial camp to which all Royal Air Force prisoners were taken – no matter where they had been shot down. Situated on the edge of a pine forest on the outskirts of Frankfurt-am-Main, it was where the Germans practised the soft/hard form of interrogation. Prisoners, still bemused by the first hours of captivity, were offered British cigarettes and Scotch whisky as the questioners gently sympathised with them, popping in the odd innocuous-sounding question about their squadron with the promise of an interview with a Red Cross official once these tedious preliminaries were concluded. (The Red Cross official of course was a German officer.) Later would come the hard interrogation following a period of solitary confinement, with questions being yelled and the prisoners threatened with dire consequences if they did not reveal what the Germans claimed they knew anyway . . . in some cases they were able to name Officers, Flight Commanders and Crews in certain

Squadrons. After induction at Dulag Luft, prisoners were allowed out of solitary into a general compound with other newly-shot-down crews and the old hands who ran the camp for the Germans. Interrogation went on again, this time by British prisoners, but most newcomers said little, believing that the old aircrew prisoners were German stooges.

flak

German anti-aircraft fire. To gain maximum coverage of a particular area of sky, the gunners swung their guns, causing the tracers to spiral upwards. A pretty but lethal sight.

Freiheit

Freedom. German motto of *Freiheit und Brot* – Freedom and Bread, was adapted by the *Recco* who turned it in its heading, into Freedom and Boat – the dearest desire of every man in the camp.

gen

Information. New prisoners were invariably milked of all gen relating to Squadron, home conditions, the state of the war and end-of-war forecasts. Some reported themselves to be scared of the hungry-eyed look of old Kriegies looking for real gen.

Gestapo

Professional 'hard men' – the enforcement arm of the Nazi party. Paid rare visits to the camps, usually after the capture of unsuccessful escapees. Much more thorough in their searches than the goons.

glop

A staple of the Kriegie diet. Glops made food go farther. In days when Red Cross parcels were shared between a large number, the glops would consist of all the meat items mushed together in a stew. In the same way all the sweet items from the parcels were glopped together, then served. An acquired taste.

goon

Black-overalled German soldiers, armed with torches, who toured the barracks, crawled underneath and poked though ashes, beds, cupboards etc, looking for contraband of any kind. Almost daily call in the huts was Goons up which was followed by a discreet flurry as Kriegies hid forbidden articles.

jawohl

Yes. Yes indeed.

Joe

A term of endearment for any prisoner who did Joe-like things. Like running round the barrack block in knee-deep snow while carrying a jug of milk in the hope that it would turn into ice cream.

This actually happened at our camp at Barth on the shores of the Baltic in mid winter. Another Joe-thing was the headfirst jump from a table-top on to the damp floor. This was done by one prisoner in the belief that he was diving into a swimming pool. The hallucination resulted from drinking home-brew, a kind of wine made from dried fruit which we received from the Red Cross. Occasionally the brew would be distilled for more effect.

Kriegie

What we all were. Short for Kriegsgefangener – Prisoner of War. Almost invariably the first words spoken to a Kriegie by his German captors were, "For you the war is over."

Lager

Camp. Usually built well away from towns. Sometimes constructed near an aerodrome or German Army camp as a source of protection – for the German war installations.

Posten

Guard. In the depths of winter while the Kriegies sat in the modest comfort of their generally reasonably warm huts, Postens would parade outside in the snow and ice.

They were sometimes provided with outer boots in which, wearing their regulation army issue boots, they stood for hours on end.

Raus

Abbreviation of *heraus*, Get out. Call by German guards to clear the barracks.

S.S.

The military version of the Gestapo, the self-acknowledged crack troops of the German war machine.

Terrorflieger

The name given to all airmen who were shot down, implying that they had been bombing towns, cities, and civilians instead of military targets. Frequently true.

Wehrmacht

German Army

Winger

Corruption of Wingman, the pilot who in a formation flew on your port or starboard wing, protecting you from above and behind and so was a special kind of guardian angel. In prison camps the enforced togetherness bred special intimacies. But very few developed into homosexual relationships. While understood by the rest of the prisoners who had all been deprived literally overnight of female companionship, they were tolerated only up to a point and blatant "love affairs" were actively discouraged. A bosom buddy.

Camp humour

APPENDIX

Copies of the *Daily Recco* are held on microfilm at the RAF Museum, Hendon. (Other items relating to Stalag Luft III are also held.)

Readers wishing to consult these copies of the *Recco* should make an appointment by telephoning the Department of Research and Information Services at the Museum on 0181 205 2266, or by writing to:

> Department of Research and Information Services
> RAF Museum
> Grahame Park Way
> Hendon
> London NW9 5LL

and quoting reference MF10121/19-20.

Thanks are due to the staff at Hendon for their assistance with archive material.